GROWING UP
BROKEN

Michele Desmond

ISBN: 979-8-9860608-2-8

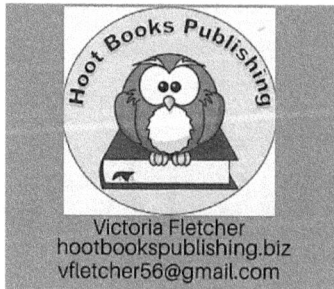

Victoria Fletcher
hootbookspublishing.biz
vfletcher56@gmail.com

Michele Desmond

Dedication

To all those surviving

Prologue

This book is completely factual.
You may not believe it all.
You will definitely believe that I am either crazy,
a survivor...
Or you may believe that I am both
and that's okay too.

I've survived.
I'm still here.
Some moments I'm only existing, yet I know there
is more "living" to come.
There will still be moments without lack of
struggle or pain....
moments where I can't breathe,
moments where I can't see or think straight...

But I will get through this....
I will survive

Walk with me through my journey

PREFACE

It was a cold November morning in1994. The sun was shining through the bedroom window. She could tell the wood stove was out and she shivered beneath the blankets.

She was alone in bed. Her husband must have been out working in the yard but she could hear nothing outside or in. The house was so still. She was thankful for the quiet. She examined the exposed beams of the bedroom and asked herself, "Which rafter shall I hang myself from?"

Today was the day she would rid herself of the insanity that had consumed her. She was nothing. She felt only numbness, even the pain from the bruises that covered her ribs and back no longer hurt. She was already dead inside; she just needed to finish the job.

As she rolled over in bed, her breath caught and she was reminded of the new lumps her head had acquired the night before as her husband came home in a drunken stupor and decided to knock around his already beaten and bruised punching bag.... The pain jolted her completely awake and she began to cry as she realized that what she thought was a bad dream was actually… HER REALITY.

Growing Up Broken

Growing Up Broken

Born in 1967 in Long Beach, California. When I was born, my father was in prison for manslaughter. He was involved in a bar fight, hit a woman in the head with a pool cue, and she died. He told the judge that he blacked out and did not remember what had happened, yet upon returning to my mother, he made it quite clear that he remembered every detail and seemed very proud of himself.

I've never come to ask her how my mother and father met, and I really didn't care to know. I just know that she was not only a victim herself of abuse, but a survivor as well.

Mom

My mother, born in 1947, had been left by her own mother, who had always wanted to be an actress. She gave birth to my mother at the age of fifteen, left her with her own parents who were in their sixties by that time, and headed to Hollywood to pursue her career.

My grandmother was successful at becoming a famous star but this lasted less than a decade, as her mental illness and excessive alcohol abuse had led her to being violent towards her many husbands and landing herself in jail for public intoxication. She had also made a few attempts on her own life during her time in the limelight.

During my mother's youth, my grandmother would come and take my mother away from her own parents, give her beautiful clothing to wear, and flaunt her around Hollywood and New York. She was photographed with her mother and whoever Mary was married to or seeing at the time; the picture ending up in the newspapers, which showed to be a functional family, was actually a world of disdain for my mother. In Wikipedia, it tells of my mother, at the age of 9, crying in the back seat as my grandmother physically abused her husband in their car.

My grandmother attempted to kill my mother; trying to throw her out of a 3-story window. She would also chase her with a butcher knife and tried to sell my mother to men in New York.

My mother stated to me in writing that my grandmother was later diagnosed with both Schizophrenia and alcoholism. She died at the age of 67.

It was strange saying our good-byes to my grandmother as she was basically a stranger to me.. All grown up, a mother myself and still broken. As she lay in her bed on oxygen and bald from the chemo, the cancer enveloped her lungs; waiting for what, an apology? She was the one who actually needed to tell my mother that she was sorry.

I really didn't know this woman, except for the few times while growing up and seeing her drunk and dysfunctional.

How my mother survived this to become so strong and to endure all the pain handed to her by her own mother and my father, I will never be able to fathom and I will always go to great lengths knowing and honoring her as one of my heroes.

In 1969, we moved to Austin, Texas, where my little sister was born. We moved close to our paternal grandmother, Bessie, who thought her son, my dad, walked on water. She absolutely adored him and would side with him on any issue that arose during small conflicts pertaining to my mother and father. My paternal grandmother was married twice; once to the love of her life, my father's dad, and then to another man who fathered my little brother, Tommy...

Tommy always took a back seat to Dad as Bessie was scorned and was still very much in love with my dad's father. Tommy got into some rat poison under the kitchen sink when he was a youth and has been brain damaged ever since. He was a kind man, always smiling and when I finally met him when I was 24, I took an instant liking to him, knowing in my heart that he would have never harmed us in the way that my father did.

My dad had opened up on occasion to my mother, telling her of the sexual contact he had with his mother while in his teens. They did not have sex but she would bring him into her bed and allow him to nurse on her breasts as if he were still an infant.

My father was a very abusive man. He would beat my mother often. He was a cocaine addict and an alcoholic. He was also bi-sexual. He would bring men home to have sex with during the time he and my mother were living together. My mother was mortified. At the age of 2, I was sexually molested by my father. When my mother confronted him about the acts, he clearly stated that any child squirming upon a man's lap would surely give him a hard-on. In the dead of night when my father was out, she packed us up, along with what she could fit into her car and left the state of Texas. She drove us to California to live closer to her relatives.

While filing for divorce, my mother had been told that her marriage was not valid. She was told that he was still married to his supposed ex-wife who's child, my half-sister, was taken care of by my mother on many occasions. Even though the marriage had been a farce, she kept his last name for herself, me, and my sister. I believe that in the seventies, people kept the underlying disgrace of abuse, any abuse, quiet so as not to raise a stir for fear of embarrassment.

My mother struggled our entire young years to provide for my younger sister and me. She put us in decent schools, took us to movies and picnics, and fed us good meals when she was eating only crackers. We wore nice clothes sewn by her own hand and she wore rags. One day, a knock came on our front door and there was our father standing in the doorway wearing a silk suit and alligator boots. Looking all shiny and clean, my father strode into the apartment trying to sweep my mother off her feet, telling her all would be different. She was smarter than that and told him to get away from us. I truly thank God for her strength.

For as long as I can remember, I wish that she had changed our names because I have NEVER wanted to have his last name. To this day, I still find myself disgusted that my own father, my own flesh and blood, defiled me at the age of two. Sometimes I still feel tainted, rotten, and ugly inside, not only because of what my father did but because of all that ensued after that in my years growing up. My father had marred me and scarred me.

This was the first occurrence of many ugly lustful experiences I would have at the hand of others until the age of 11 where I would then decide that was what love was. That was how I would show others that I was their loyal, loving friend. Sex became as normal to me as breathing air. I offered sex to my friends, both male and female, no differently than someone opening the door to relatives, asking them to have a seat, and offering them a cold drink. I remained this way throughout my teen years and into my early 20s until I met my sons' father.

In 1971, when I was a mere 4 years of age, we were living in the city of Long Beach, California. I attended a Christian preschool.

During that entire year, I was sexually molested by a female preschool teacher. I remember that I was not one of the children that played with others; all I can remember was that I sat by a tree most days and watched the ants make a home for themselves as the earth rose.

I was a sexual toy to this woman. I do not recall her face at all. She would take me into an empty classroom; lay me down with my lower body under a teacher's desk and my head sticking out of the front, while she would have her way with my body. I believe that I felt this was wrong, yet she was so tender with her touch that I think I might have psychologically believed she cared about me. This, my mother recalled, was when I began sucking my thumb and continued to do so until the age of 12.

While growing up, I never remember getting hugs from my mother. She was not the nurturing type but a very intelligent individual and I believe she showed her love for us by the picnics we had, the gifts that we were given at every holiday, and when she took us on outings to the movies or picnics. This is how she was raised.

My mother and I spoke about it at length one day and she stated that by being raised by her grandparents, who were well into their sixties, watching television together in the living room and having dinner at the table was the type of love she received. In other words, more or less, fellowshipping with the family was her way of knowing she was loved.

So in return, we were never hugged, kissed, read bedtime stories, or told that we were loved. I do remember being told that she wishes she would have never had us because parenthood was very difficult for her and being a single parent was harder than she ever thought she could imagine. When she was angry with me, I recall her stating that I was just like my father, told that I would never amount to anything, and she wished I was never born. That broke my heart, which in turn became a huge wall between us, and I felt like a loser, unwanted, unloved, and despised because I was "just like my father" whom she loathed.

In 1974, I was sexually molested by a black man who lived in our apartment complex. He almost got to my sister but I put myself in front of her... I was seven and my sister was five.

We lived in Huntington Beach in a huge apartment complex. I remember riding my big wheel through the halls and around the complex. I was in the second grade at the time and while not in school, my sister and I were being sat by a woman in the complex while my mother worked. My little sister and I would go to the top of the apartment building to sunbathe. This sun area was the size of a small baseball field. On each wall was a large sliding door giving access to the sunning area and she and I were the only ones there.

One day, we noticed a man of color walking around the sun-bathing area. I remember feeling very uncomfortable and told my little sister to gather her things and that we needed to go home. As we did so, I viewed the man open one of the sliders and begin to walk towards us. I told my little sister to run as I was right behind her and to get to the elevator that was closest to us. As the elevator door opened, the man had caught up to us. I shoved my sister into the elevator as he grabbed my arm. I knew something bad would happen to the both of us and I did not want my little sister to be harmed.

I attempted with every ounce of my being to get away from him by kicking, hitting, screaming, and crying. He lifted me up, pulled down my bathing suit bottoms, and began shoving his fingers inside of me, groping me, and then letting me fall to the concrete floor just outside of the elevator. He then turned and walked off as if he was taking a casual stroll. I waited for the elevator to return to the top level, entered it, and collapsed. When the elevator reached the ground level, I picked myself up and ran as fast as I could to our apartment to tell my mother. My little sister had run home to tell my mother. When I got to our apartment, I ran into my mother's arms and told her what had happened while crying and aching from what had transpired.

My mother grabbed a butcher knife, grabbed my arm, and took me to the man's apartment where he lived with his mother. She banged on the door, yelling at the top of her lungs. The man's mother answered the door and her son was standing just behind her. I hid behind my mother as she told them that she was not going to call the cops, that she wouldn't waste the court system's time, that she would take care of it herself and kill him and it would be over. I wasn't sure how my mother knew this guy but came to realize that this person was a neighbor of our babysitter. My mother never had us return to that sitter or the area.

One day, our neighbor stopped by for a visit with my mother who had befriended her. This woman was African American. Back in those days there was still a lot of racial tension, especially at our particular building. Our neighbor came over to our apartment for a chat one day and when she left our place, a different neighbor came by later to tell my mother that this was not a good thing. She was often called a "Nigger lover" after that and my mother made the decision to move away from this community of abuse and hatred. My mother didn't discriminate against anyone, unless they were a threat to her family.

In 1976, we resided in a duplex in Downey, California. My sister and I had puppies named Whiskey and Ginger. We took piano lessons and Mom had a garden in our backyard. Looking back on it now, it seems that we were maintaining a pretty normal family life until the evenings came that my mother went to school or out with friends. We were kept by different sitters and I recall one gal who had a party at our apartment. She and her friends would blow pot smoke into our faces to get us high, while continuing to party. I remember one night walking into my mother's room and seeing my babysitter and a man having sex in my mom's bed. I didn't remember much of that year but going to school, being a tomboy, and not having many friends. The neighbor gal had asked me if I wanted to spend the night one evening and I accepted. That evening she came on to me and that was the last time we spoke. I'm glad we didn't live there for very long.

We moved from the duplex in 1977 to Lakewood, California. We moved into a huge house with three bedrooms and a fireplace. It felt like a mansion to me. My bedroom was the largest, set at the rear of the house. It was adorned with yellow flowers and three windows to let in the sunlight during any part of the day. My sister's room was the smallest of the three and was a beautiful lavender color with wood shutters on her windows. Mom's room was at the front of the house and was a bland setting but functional enough for a person who was rarely there. It held a bed, a dresser, and a closet. I do not recall any curtains or a picture on the wall.

I attended a public school about a half mile from home. I was not a pleasant student. As a matter of fact, I was quite a bully to other kids on the playground. Tether ball was my game and I would not be defeated. All the aggression I had was taken out on this ball on a rope. I tore into it with all my might. I challenged anyone to this rigorous game and I won each and every time. People did not want to play with me anymore so I took up four-square and was plainly an ass to anyone around me..

In class, I was the court jester: flatulating or making loud, crazy sounds that would break out a riot of laughing from the rest of the class. My teacher did not like me at all, and I didn't blame him a bit. I sat in the last row all the way in the far back right corner of the classroom. I remember him being, or at least stating that he was, a man of God. He and I would talk after school sometimes about my behavior. When I really wanted to make a good impression on him, I would sit quietly and draw pretty pictures during class so that I wasn't in trouble all of the time. On one of my bad days, the teacher kept me after school. When all the kids had left the classroom, he locked the door. I was told to sit on a chair next to his desk. We spoke of my crass behavior and he inquired as to why I was constantly acting out. I literally had no idea. You see, I think I had shoved all the shit I had gone through previously in my life and just became a jerk. I was guarded and mean. I had stopped dressing like a girl, always wearing corduroy jeans, t-shirts, and dirty sneakers. I rode skateboards and my bike everywhere.

I was once hit by a car, only to pick my bike up and run away with it when the owner of the car tried to come to my aid.

On this bad day after school, the teacher began yelling at the top of his lungs at me.

I do not remember anything he said, only that I tried to run to the door to get out of the classroom as he lunged for me and grabbed my leg. We both fell hard on the classroom floor. I kicked him in his face and was able to get to the door, unlock it, and bolt out. Days after that, I mostly sat in the office or with the principal doing my school work. My mother told me that the principal said the teacher was not a good teacher, but in reality, looking at it now, I was the bad egg, not my teacher.

I remember that my favorite bands at the time were Van Halen, The Beatles, Wings, and The Bee Gees. I also had a huge crush on a short-lived singer by the name of Leif Garrett. I returned home from school one day, only to find all of my favorite records melted into odd shapes by leaving my collection lying just under the windows of my room. I remember being very sad, as the music was, for me, a way of escaping. Reading was important as well. I could escape my own reality for a while in books. Outside of this universe, I was uncomfortable, ugly, and full of hatred..

My hair was short, my two front teeth were large, and I looked very much like a boy or horse.. My smile was crooked and my face was full of freckles.

My sister and I were placed in a softball league. I had a HUGE crush on Steve Garvey at the time. He was a left-handed first baseman for a professional baseball team. So I had to be the left-handed, first baseman on the softball team that I was assigned to, "The Blue Angels". We sucked! This was a very good sport for my little sister, though, as her team went on to state finals and came home with shiny trophies.

My neighbor, Paul and his mom, would let me go over to their house to view their "pets" which were huge turtles in their backyard. They kept their grass waist high and full of reeds for the turtles to live in and dine on. They were the biggest turtles I had ever seen. Paul would let me clean his room, as he was quite a messy person, and I could keep all of the money I would find on the floor for doing this task. I was always happy to clean his room because it allowed me to buy candy or treats for my little sister and myself when the ice cream truck arrived.

In 1978, sixth grade rolled around and my mother placed me in a new school. This was a Christian school that housed our church as well and was not too much farther from our home on Oliva Street. The new school sat just on the edge of Lakewood and Long Beach, California. I liked my teacher, Mr. Cook. He was smart and funny and also played the horn for the Los Angeles Lakers' basketball team. He took our whole class to see him play in the band and watch the Lakers play. I remember one day we had a spelling bee. My word was "PIECE." I had always had a hard time remembering if the "I" came before "E" or vice versa with this word. I spelled the word incorrectly, "PIECE" and I was out of the game. I was pissed off, acted out, and was sent to the principal's office. Back in the day when I was growing up, spanking was allowed in schools. And this principal had holes in his paddle! I didn't remember ever acting out after that day.

I was a part of the chess club after school and my grades were all A's and B's. I think I was happy at this school. I had a few friends. My best friend was named Dena. Nothing bad ever happened when school was in session or when we attended church. I believe I was moderately content and I know that I had settled down after that spanking, so the rest of the school year was fun and uneventful.

On one particular weekend day, I was walking with my little sister to the corner store to get some candy and we were nearing our church/school. We noticed a parked car in front of our church and we saw the back of someone's head in the car. As we walked adjacent to the car, we see a man who was masturbating in front of our church, plainly defiling our school and our church. I have no idea what was in this man's head but it freaked me out! I grabbed little sister's hand and made her walk faster towards the corner store. I remember feeling disgusted having seen that. I felt ashamed. I felt lonely and I felt unprotected. All I know is I was getting my sister the hell out of there. Maybe there wasn't any protection for me but I was sure as hell going to keep protecting my little sister for as long as I could.

That summer, I was very industrious. My mother sold products made by a "pyramid company." I would take her best car soaps and rags to wash cars around the neighborhood to make money and I would mow lawns as well. I would often take the money and spend it on my little sister at the candy store or our favorite restaurant to get a hot fudge cake sundae. Bob's Big Boy was a family household name. Mom would come home tired so often that we would have take-out from this place just about every week.

When my mother did have spare time, she had a most interesting hobby. She made the most beautiful candles. I would sit and watch the process of this craft and admired her for doing so.

We had a large back yard and my mother and sister would have picnics on the weekends.

My period came during our stay at the Oliva house. My mother gave me books to read. She did not go through this process verbally with me as I believe this was how she learned about herself as well.

She then took me to see my birth doctor, Dr. A. He had me hold a mirror to my privates to watch him point out all of my female parts with a Q-tip and to tell me how each part worked and what they were for. I was mortified and hated my mother for taking me here to do that. She sat in the room while it was happening. Why did she feel this was necessary?

Dena, my best friend, and I began hanging out all the time. Her mother was never home, so we hung out there often. My best friend and I began to experiment with one another sexually and even though, in the back of my mind, I knew this was going to lead to a bad end, I went along with it because that was what friends did, right? Dena then takes me to her new boyfriend's house. This guy gave us beer to drink and pot to smoke and we became pretty obliterated.

We all ended up in his bedroom. I remember being extremely nervous and we all laid down together on the floor. He is making out with her. I'm nervous and I look away. He proceeds to kiss and fondle me.

I didn't remember my best friend being there anymore. But then I do remember her being by my side, her eyes were closed, and somewhere in the back of my mind, it feels like she passed out... I didn't know. I can't remember if she was there or not, but this guy continued to get physical with me, and kissing me and putting his hands and body on me, and I kept yelling and pleading for him to STOP! I then began screaming for him to get off of me and when he finished the act he had committed, I ran into the bathroom and locked the door and cried. Blood was dripping down my legs so I cleaned myself up as best I could. I didn't understand then but my virginity had been lost to a vile person committing a vile act. I was so afraid to leave the bathroom because I would have to see him again and Dena never came to my aid. What the hell had just happened? It's kind of surreal and all cloudy. It looks hazy when I try and actually see it in my mind's eye. I don't even remember running home. I hadn't realized at that time that I had just been raped....

In 1979, we moved to Signal Hill. This was on the Pacific Coast Highway of Long Beach, California. I started 7th grade at a Baptist school. I rode the public bus to and from school.

On this route, I passed a fast-food restaurant and began stopping in there a few times a week to grab a snack.

I became friends with the assistant manager there and soon we became lovers. I was 12 years old and he was 17.

I had my own room and my sister shared a room with my mother. He and I would go to my place and engage in sex quite frequently. He was in a rock band at the time we were seeing each other. I loved going with him to watch his band play Cheap Trick songs in his friend's garage. He was the lead guitarist and singer and I was lost in the music, fell in love with it actually, because it would take me away from everything I thought about all that was hurtful. I think I loved him with the best ability a 12-year-old could.

One day my mom catches us in the act of having sex. She ran Alan out of our apartment and thrust me into our bathtub of extremely hot water. Now I didn't know if this made my mother think that the hot water would kill the sperm or if it was some sort of punishment. I'm not sure. I do know that it seared my skin and I was in pain.

After the scalding bath, she had me dress and led me to Alan's house and we met his parents. My mother was furious and yelling. We were banned from ever seeing each other again and my mother asked for a transfer... an opening came up in Illinois and she took the job!

I was fighting tooth and nail to stay in California. My grandmother was there to help get us to the airport after my mom came home from errands.

I ran to the end of the block near our apartments and proceeded to call a friend of mine, John, who was a platonic friend from school.

As I was crying on the phone, I was suddenly grabbed by my hair, pay phone left dangling in the air, and literally dragged back to my apartment. My grandmother was screaming at me to get inside, hair still in hand. As she let go of my hair, I ran to the bathroom and locked the door. While Grandma banged on the door, I tried the best I could to climb out the tiny bathroom window, to no avail, so that I could run away... but to where?

1979-1980 Illinois

Upon moving to Illinois, I began to have this reoccurring dream that lasted about 4 years....

My Dream

I sat in a corner, the cold and unfamiliar dark arms wrapped around my knees for warmth and comfort, locked in what seemed to be a huge and empty warehouse.

It's pitch black. I'm frightened and exhausted..

There's a box at the opposite end of the room and when my eyes get tired and start to close, I'm jolted awake and see that the box has moved closer, growing larger, getting ready to envelop and consume me, leaving me as nothing.

I know this box will be my fate.

The hours pass by and each time I blink my eyes, the box has drawn nearer.

It has become immense and so very overwhelming. My panic attack sets in and just before the box envelops me, I wake up in a cold sweat.

I remember homeroom. I remember that in sewing class I would walk by my other classmates and poke them with a needle. Not hard, but enough for them to holler out. My nicknames at that school were "Thunder Thighs" and "Psycho." I liked "Psycho" so much that I had a ball shirt screen printed with the word on it. I wasn't ashamed of being "mad." It kept me from feeling any real emotion. Anger was all I knew then.

I was one of the least popular kids at my school. I was not pretty, my hair had turned red from the winter months, and I was a big girl. I remember getting into a fight with another girl, not remembering who or why, and blacking out. When I came to, I was sitting in the principal's office. The girl had been sent home, or to the hospital, I do not recall. I was told that I beat her in the head with my books and she had to leave because of the wounds she had received from this beating.

Why we fought I haven't a clue. I'm sure I was suspended but not kicked out of the school, as I returned to school the following week. No one really bothered me after that but I still had the nickname of "Psycho" and it stuck even through the eighth grade.

I rode my bike everywhere in La Grange. Even in the wintertime, I would ride my bike in the snow to deliver papers when I had a paper route. My mother would drive me around most of the time when it became too hard to ride my bike. I liked my route and enjoyed the money when I got paid.

One night, while my mother was out for the evening, the power went out in our apartment. My sister and I lit candles and hung out together in the living room. For some stupid reason, I thought of a brilliant idea to show my sister a trick I had seen on television. I ran to the bathroom, grabbed a can of hairspray, and aimed the can at a candle. The fire it created was very cool to me. I aimed the can closer to my sister and the hair spray widened out towards my sister's face and burned her bangs and eyebrows off. I was horrified that this had happened and took care of her to the best of my ability until my mother came home to help her and discipline me. I truly did feel bad for what happened to my sister but I think she felt I had done this on purpose.

There were so many places to ride through the forests and over to my school. I befriended a girl named Jennifer, nicknamed "Bubble Butt" and we rode everywhere. When Jennifer and I weren't together, I would ride bikes with my friend Jimmy. He and I had taken up a sexual relationship and I would ride for miles to his house to see him when his mother was out working the night shift. One evening on occasion, after having sex, he grabbed me and pulled me down onto our knees on the carpeted floor to pray for mercy because he had failed to "pull out." Soon after that evening, our encounters became farther apart as the fear of my getting pregnant was terrifying to both of us.

Jennifer lived in an elite neighborhood that held a vast amount of huge and beautiful Victorian houses. Jennifer had her good moments and her bad towards me. She would be kind to me at times when we hung out and rode our bikes together.

Jennifer hated her parents for reasons she never discussed with me. I do recall that her mother was constantly on her back about speaking correctly and behaving in a manner that pleased her parents and that did not sit well with Jennifer. But when we were at her home and her parents were gone, she would walk me up to her attic or basement and then push me into the rooms and lock me in by her strength on the other side of the door. I have since then been a bit claustrophobic and do not care to enter those types of rooms alone. After the second time being locked in the basement, I rammed through the door and we fought like cats and ended whatever type of friendship that was deemed.

I was such a tomboy while in junior high and at night, a few friends and I would play flashlight tag in the dark. We would climb trees and onto garages while playing tag. One evening, I was getting close to being tagged and went to the edge of a garage that I was on. I was facing a tree that I was going to jump onto. I backed up several feet and ran to jump onto the tree, only to fall short of my destination and onto my back at the base of the tree. My back was too sore to continue on with the game, so I rode my bike a little over the two miles needed to return to my home. I entered my home and went to bed straight away.

The next morning came and I was not able to get out of bed. Something was terribly wrong with my back. My mother took me to the hospital emergency room and they took x-rays. When the films came back, the doctor informed my mom that I had fractured my lumbar spine at levels L-2 and L-3. They put me into a body cast which went from just under my breasts down to just above my hips. I was to wear this cast for 90 days and return for the removal of the cast, get new X-rays, and move on to physical therapy.

Having this cast on, I was only able to fit into my corduroy jeans and large flannel button down shirts. I looked even bigger than before and was teased constantly. This only hardened my attitude towards my classmates even more and I became an angry recluse. I still hung out with the older kids in high school in the evenings and still rode my bike.

I didn't let the cast get me down too much so I could still smoke pot and listen to my favorite musical artists: Jimmy Hendrix, Black Sabbath, and Pink Floyd. I did settle down a little while not being able to play tag at night or tennis while in school.

When I had to shower, I would tie a large black trash bag around my cast to keep it from getting it wet. However, my cleavage allowed the water to run down the front of my cast and it became soft and began to smell after some time. I made the personal decision after 6 weeks to cut the cast off of my body with a pair of scissors as much as I could. Eventually, I had the cast off entirely. The transformation of my body was astounding. I actually had an hourglass shape and had lost quite a few inches off of my back and waist.

The school year had come to an end and I graduated from the eighth grade. My mother bought me a beautiful white summer dress that came with a white, short lace type jacket. I had white low-heeled shoes that I wore with the dress and I was beautiful. Middle school was over and summer came again. Mom had enough of Illinois and decided to move us back to California.

California Life 1980

Upon returning to California from Illinois, we moved to a town called Santa Ana and lived in a large community of condominiums. I was enrolled in high school as a freshman. I felt out of sorts and was shy at first but then made friends, all of whom partied, of course. I befriended a gal named Carol. She and I were close friends and we had experimented sexually with one another. She also introduced me to a world even darker than the previous life I had already led. The new drugs she introduced me to were different substances and pills of all sorts: black beauties, pink hearts, Quaaludes (hallucinogens), and blotter acid. Back in the 80s, things were easy to obtain. There was an actual magazine, very similar to a typical Reader's Digest, that allowed ANYONE to purchase pills of various sorts to have delivered right to our door. Carol and I became drug dealers.

Blotter acid was old school compared to the type of acid there is on the market currently. This was called blotter acid because it was made from a large sheet of paper with serrated edges consisting of small squares about the size of your thumb. Each little square held a Disney character like Donald Duck, Goofy, and Mickey Mouse. Each tab, or square, was blotted with a drop of acid per square. The sheet was then carefully cut into pieces keeping each square, or blotter, intact.

These were then distributed to Carol and me and after trying the acid for the first time, we then were given the ability to sell these and make extra money as well as the money we were earning from the pills.

I remember distinctly, the evening we took our first hit of acid. We were at a friend of Carol's house and we sat down to have a beer, pop the blotter tab, and listen to the band RUSH.

When we began to trip, the world became so colorful. I would move my hand in front of my face and I would see colorful tracers following my hand. It was a trip to trip! I found my new happy drug!! Then Carol's friend started a very eerie and mostly silent film called 'Eraser Head." I still look back and remember that night being pretty epic in a sinister way.

After school, I began working part time at our closest fast-food restaurant as a hostess and a window cashier. Back in those days, the girls were made to wear mid-thigh one piece, zip up dresses and nylon stockings. I would take the order, give the customers their number, and carry their food tray with their order on it to them directly. When the customer left, I would clean up the table they sat at and sweep and mop the floors as well as wash the windows when it was slow.

As I promoted my way up the fast-food ladder, I then became the window order taker as well as the hostess. One day, as I was working the window, a customer made an order then drove up to the window. Lord, I had never seen such a beautiful boy in my life; in person, that is. He reminded me of a golden-haired god played in a movie of Roman times. He told me that he worked just across the street as a mechanic and we were very excited when we exchanged numbers and I knew this was the beginning of something big, yet I did not realize just how large this "something" was going to turn out to be.

I interviewed for the position and was hired on the spot. I left the fast-food joint to work across the street at the car repair shop as the "secretary." I did well in my work and was able to see this creature of heaven every day. He and I eventually became boyfriend and girlfriend and at any given moment, we could steal a kiss in between repair work or on our lunch breaks together.

The shop that I worked at was a small repair shop, holding only two cars at a time. The front office was a decent size, able to hold a few customers waiting for their cars to be repaired and my large desk in which I took calls and messages, typed out repair orders, and filed. I liked my job and made three times the minimum wage, so I was stoked and felt I had the dream life where I could hang with my guy and make money doing the work that I had come to enjoy immensely.

Next to the front office where I sat, there was a very large break room. It contained three couches, a pool table, and a large lunch table with many chairs; and behind the door there was a video camera. I enjoyed my small breaks and lunch time as my golden boy and I would find time to steal a kiss and a little more when the time felt right and we had our privacy. One of the couches had a fold out bed. After a brief month of simple kissing and petting, we went to the next level and began having sex on our lunch breaks. This became a regular thing and the owner of the car shop did not have any complaints at all, which surprised me.

A few months into my career at the shop, I introduced my friend Carol to everyone at the shop, including my boyfriend. Not too long after her meeting with everyone, she chose to partake in the sexual encounters with the men at the shop and, finally, with my boyfriend, which hurt me but did not surprise me. When I found out that all these sexual encounters had been taped, I was shocked. I decided that I did not want to have a boyfriend that would go out on me. I was later told that this boy was a conduit into this world of pornography and the shop was basically a cover up for the intent of making the kind of money that pornography would bring in.

Just prior to my leaving this shop, I was introduced to men who had A LOT of money, drove Jaguars and Corvettes, wore silk suits and fantastic cologne. They spoke to me about leaving the shop and jumping into a life of luxury and money. They took me to fancy restaurants in Hollywood, took me shopping at expensive stores, bought me beautiful outfits and fur coats, as well as very seductive lingerie.

I have to be honest, this frightened me but it also had my heart racing to see what was around the corner in this new chapter of my life. I made a ton of money which they put into an account which had their name on it as well as mine.

I was not allowed to touch the money until I had completed a few weeks of instructed hotel encounters and when the money was drawn out of the account, little by little, it was to dine at the restaurants, buy new clothing and lingerie, and be introduced to an even new, and better in my opinion, drug that took away any inhibition of keeping my clothes on and participating in sex with the client or clients, that I was introduced to.

I was quite the commodity as I was sexually interested in both men and women and I learned as I went with each encounter and became quite good at the roles in which I played to satisfy the customer and make a freaking ton of money. One night in particular, I was handed $700.00 just for playing a dominant figure in a threesome. The couple loved being told what to do and they carried out every act that I seductively whispered in their ears. I felt empowered and loved playing the dominant role. (This role carried into my life later on in years, but we will get to that in a few chapters later on). I was then taken to houses at the top of Beverly Hills and Hollywood to watch orgies and sometimes engage in them. I was given drugs that induced a sexual appetite I did not know existed. I remember being scared shitless at each new endeavor or party but not only that, it was absolutely exhilarating at the same time and sex became an addiction for me. I didn't even give a shit about the cameras anymore. This was an addiction that I never wanted to let go of.

This became my life. Life was about sex, friendship was about sex, love was about sex... SEX WAS LOVE...

During this time in my freshman year of being a teenager, I was always away for such long periods of time and this made my mother a nervous wreck. Whenever I did make it home, I returned stoned out of my mind and completely incoherent. She was afraid for my life.

When my mother saw me come home in these repeated states of mind, she decided that I needed to enter a psychiatric hospital in Cerritos, California, to fix my addictive behavior and get me back into school. I had a hard time with this as my exciting world had come to a close, but there was also a huge part of me that was ready to pull my brain out of that fog and find out who I was as a sober person.

My mother thought that I was mentally ill. Her mother had been diagnosed as a Schizophrenic and mother feared that I had the same affliction. I had not opened up to her about all the things I had engaged in prior to going into this hospital.

During my time at this hospital in 1981, my IQ was tested. I was told that my scores were way above average and given courses to challenge me. I aced every class and I even enjoyed learning. I actually acquired a thirst for knowledge and the challenges that it brought with each lesson. I remember there were times when I never wanted to leave. I felt safe here, even normal at times. I had put my past life behind me and this felt good.

One afternoon, while eating lunch in the cafeteria with my unit and my favorite therapist, Terry, we were all cracking jokes and everyone was in a happy mood at my table. Terry told a joke so funny that I spit my root beer out of my mouth and some even shot out of my nose as well. It hurt terribly, but I laughed even harder.

Laughing was so good, I had forgotten that it was okay to be a kid again, and this terrified me as well.

I really did not know who I was, what I was, or if I wanted to live or die. Life did not matter to me as I was such an unhappy person full of doubt, chaos, and destructiveness. I hated being alive. I hated being me.

I began getting into trouble and was sent to a "lock down" unit for a few days at each incident that I misbehaved. While in this unit, the other kids that were in trouble along with me would act in ways that were so destructive. We would snort our packets of sugar or Sweet and Low, or we would choke ourselves out so severely as to cause a seizure just to have some sort of entertainment, as we did not have televisions, let alone anything else while in this unit. My first attempt at suicide was by trying to hang myself with a tied-up sheet to the water sprayer in the ceiling that would go off if there was a fire in the unit. I was tied to the bed and sedated. When I regained a better attitude, I was release back into the regular unit.

When my class courses became mundane and I was no longer challenged, I became mischievous and started getting into trouble. A close eye was kept on me. I became the Michele of the past and gained the affections of a boy. The other girls had as well. I was not an accomplice to their deceptiveness, but I am sure that I did not help matters much when I took the reins of sneaking on arms and belly down the hallways to the guys' rooms that were across the hall.

There was a hall monitor that would sit and monitor the hallway while reading. Now, in my current years, I find that reading helps me to fall asleep and it did just that for the hall monitor. Slowly and methodically, we would all make it to our destinations and have sex. The old Michele was back. I was then tied to the bed and given sedatives. I then began more intensive therapy and was released back into the regular ward.

My therapy at this hospital was actually helpful. I wasn't so much into speaking with an adult who read from a textbook to label me and put me on psych medication. The therapy that touched my heart, lowered my blood pressure, and instantly calmed me was MUSIC therapy. I had electrodes attached to me in various places to log my BP, pulse, and whatever else they were working on with me. Then they turned on music that I had chosen to listen to. My favorite sounds were of rivers running, wind chimes, the wind, and the ocean. Soothing sounds took everything away but feeling drugged with a new and great addiction.

At the end of my stay at College Hospital, I met with a female counselor and we began meeting with my mom and sister. Our family therapy, to me, was a joke. I was not in touch with my feelings and what had happened to me in my past that my mother didn't know about was not shared.

I talked the talk and walked the walk just to get out of that place. My mother set the ground rules on how I was to behave and act when I came home. I agreed to them, knowing that I would not do as she wanted, and we all signed a "contract" acknowledging that we would all behave accordingly. When I was set free of the psychiatric hospital, I reverted back to my old ways and I have no doubt that it tore my mother apart to see that I had just manipulated my way out of the hospital, only to go back to who and what I was prior to being put into the psych ward.

Back home in Santa Ana

Carol and I were in a large department store and back then, there were woven bags to obtain and put the items in that people wanted to purchase, as these stores did not have shopping carts. A few times a month, Carol and I would enter our favorite department store, load the bag with what we wanted, and walked right out of the store with the bag and items in hand. One day we were caught and taken to the security office where they counted up the prices of the items to determine how much in dollars we had stolen. If the amount went over $400.00, we would be charged with a felony. If under $400.00, then it would be considered a misdemeanor. I had several charms inside my shoes, which they did not search and my total amount stolen came to just under $400.00 and Carol and I were given citations, our mothers were called to pick us up, and we had a court date to see the judge.

I was put on probation for two years. My court demands stipulated that I was to stay in school, not do drugs, and complete community service. One weekend I was to do community service, I was on drugs and tested positive on the spot. My mother was called to come get me and I went back to court for violating my court order. I was then put into juvenile hall to serve a few weeks. My mother would come to see me and I pleaded with her to get me out of there. In this place, I resided with child killers, felons, and a host of others with crimes committed that were far greater than mine. I was released back to my home and put on probation for a longer period of time, only to violate my probation repeatedly.

On one occasion when I was serving six months, I was stabbed in the head with a large serving spoon for provoking a person during clean up time after lunch was served. If you know this, you will understand that a head wound bleeds profusely. I screamed as the hot blood spewed from the back of my head, my vision left me in both eyes and I had such a loud ringing in my head it tuned out anything the paramedics were saying to me. There was a hospital in the same complex that housed the juvenile hall and I was given seven staples in my head and sent back to the ward. The girl that had stabbed me was 17 and sent to adult jail to be sentenced.

When I was released, I was sent home, returned back to my high school, and given the same stipulations for probation as before. I tried to behave but my choices were poor and my common sense was very lacking. I befriended a boy in high school who introduced me to others in his group of friends. They were all potheads and I fit right in. I really liked this boy, Chris, and so did this other chick, Pam. We eventually fought over him, yet the strangest thing occurred— we became best friends, and soon after, lovers.

Chris was our boy toy and other boys became so as well. I stayed in school and did my work so that I could hang out with Pam and the boys we had strung along. Pam had the most intense eyes and I could not handle the depth in which she would gaze at me. Our relationship was intense as I had never played the part of being the submissive in a sexual relationship. Pam liked to drink more than get high. I, however, did not enjoy drinking and when I did, I made an ass out of myself. I recall a lot of fighting, peeing on the front yard of a person's house that I didn't know, in broad daylight. The owner came out to see if I was okay and I mumbled that I was while I finished relieving myself on his front lawn.

Another time, I remember walking through my condominium complex, laid down in the alley, and passed out. A friend of mine found me hours later and I was hardly wearing any clothing. He walked me to my home and my mother put me to bed right away and then called my probation officer to let her know what had happened so that I could get help or go back to juvenile hall. It was up to my probation officer to make that call so I was sent to a drug rehab in Dana Point, California.

Dana Point, California 1982/83

This drug rehabilitation program was a freaking joke. The facility was a converted motel complex into housing for drug offenders such as me. We cooked our own meals, cleaned after ourselves, and were managed at a thrift shop attached to our facility to sell used clothing and shoes to help fund this rehab center.

Our beds were old, filthy, and creaked when sitting or lying on them. These beds had buttons on the mattresses and would tear our sheets when we made our beds up. The food was sent to us from a local food bank. Our water was filthy and tasted like sulfur. We were rarely supervised; however, our facility was patrolled by the highway patrol and local authorities many times daily to keep us in line. The cops would stop in often and spoke with the few counselors that were attending to us.

Our school work was sub-par and we lived in filth. It was a horrible place to be and I did not gain anything whatsoever with my sobriety, counseling, or schooling.

One evening, as I was preparing for bed, I climbed into my bed and the button had cut right through the sheet and ripped my knee open. I watched as the blood seeped out of my knee and went to the office immediately for medical care. As I entered the office, I saw no one there. I went to the rear of the office where the supervisor was housed and walked in without knocking. There is where I found this counselor shooting up a black substance called heroine. I put my hands over my mouth and backed out of the room. The counselor came out after me and told me to go straight to bed. While doing so, I watched how he fell out of sorts and slumped to the floor.

I went back to my room and cleaned myself up to the best of my ability. I knew that I needed stitches and by all means, should have called 9-1-1 for my knee and to have the authorities deal with the counselor. I was too frightened to do either so I wrapped up my knee with a hand towel and cried myself to sleep.

The next day, the counselor called me into his office, threatened to cause bodily damage to me if I told the cops who would come by what I had seen. He then looked at my knee and put sterilized strips on it, thinking this would help. I have a very large and long scar to this day from that incident. My mother was not even called regarding this matter.

Relationships were not allowed at this rehab, naturally. However, with the lack of supervision at all times, relationships ran rampant. Some were caught and some were not. I was one of the couples that were caught.

When a couple is caught at this facility, the boys and girls were disciplined in a way that was both embarrassing and humiliating to both parties. The boys had their heads shaved bald and had to wear a sign which held one word on it, "OFFENDER." Then the boys were made to wear the sign on the sidewalk next to the highway in which the facility was located.

The girls were made to wear nylon hose over their heads so that none of our hair was visible. We were to wear large clothing from the thrift store inside out and also to wear a sign that held the word, "OFFENDER" on it as well. We were then made to pace the sidewalk holding our signs for three days between breakfast and lunch and then from dinner to dusk.

After being disciplined at this bullshit place considered a drug rehabilitation, our parents would be called and we were kicked out of the program.

When my mother came to pick me up, she was so pissed off that she refused to hear anything I had to say about the manager shooting up and didn't even show concern towards my knee. She was done with me. She drove close to our house, found the nearest police station, walked me into the facility, handed me off to a cop, and said straight out, "Take her, I don't want her."

The cops did not know what to do with me so I was put into a cell and they contacted the nearest half-way house to hold me there until they could find adequate housing for me.

This halfway house was dirty and dilapidated. It consisted of a house counselor that, I could feel, had no interest in helping the girls overcome any issues. I feel she was only there for a paycheck and a free place to live. We were made to clean and do yard work while biding our time as to where we would be headed next. While there, I contracted lice and had to scour myself from head to toe to clear this disgusting ailment. That's how filthy this house was…

A few weeks into staying at this half way home, I was passed on back into juvenile hall, which was, by far, better than being at that disgusting halfway house or drug rehab in Dana Point. I rested up and went back to school within the facility.

Upon returning to court to see the judge, I saw that my mother was there as well. She addressed the court and told them that she no longer wanted me home and she gave her consent to become a "ward of the state."

It was very hard to hear my mother tell the officers at the police station that she didn't want me and then again to the judge in court. I knew I had failed her as she had told me on many occasions while growing up that I was just like my father and would never make anything of myself. She also stated to my sister and me that had she wished we were never born.

Years later, when we spoke to her about this, she went over her reasoning for that statement with us. She told us that she never wanted us born because it was too hard for her and us to survive in a one parent family without a father to help raise us. It doesn't matter how a parent puts that into context or gives a reason why they would say that, it still crushed us both.

However, looking back, and having been where she once was, I can see why she felt that way and I no longer hold that against her as I feel this world is too fucked up for any child to grow up in this society with the world being like it is these days, even with a two-parent family.

A Ward of the State

As a ward of the state, the court could mandate any rules, regulations, and care agencies to house me. I was sent to an all-girl's group home in Ramona, California. The group home, or homes, were located throughout the city of Ramona.

There were six houses in which to reside. The first house was a beginner home. It housed six girls and two female counselors. There were rules that had to be followed: cleaning the house, speaking openly on a daily basis, and keeping a log that was perused through by the House Moms. We also had mandatory group house meetings and one-on-one counseling. Our schooling was held on the campus of the facility centrally located between each house.

We had the typical classes that a regular school had, yet our group meetings were much larger due to the six houses that contained each girl. Also, our physical education was more in depth and I appreciated this because it helped me get into better shape physically and I gained better self-esteem as my health improved.

This was my house of refuge, one I never took for granted. My favorite counselor at this house was named Mom Shirley. She was an amazing person, full of compassion and understanding. She never judged and was always there to talk to, no matter the context. She was an excellent cook and my most favorite dish that she would make for us was blackened chicken.

Every girl in this home had come from an abusive or neglectful family. We all shared common stories but needed our own distinct type of therapy. Our group meetings were meant to get to know one another and bring up any issues that were related to our "house" issues either with one another, our assigned jobs within the house, or to open up so that we could learn how to trust others and to become socially adaptable.

When each girl was content with their surroundings and had fulfilled the house rules and regulations on a consistent basis, they were transferred to another house. This transition was a graduation of sorts, to the next level of responsibility, to a new level of healing and faith, or trust, in others.

I, however, had a huge tantrum when I was spoken to about moving to a level which would take me out of the care on Mom Shirley. I regressed in my growth which allowed me to stay longer in this home while the other girls moved on.

The House Mothers would stay overnight a few days a week, then the house would gain another matriarch for the remaining days. This made for a close and trusting relationship with these women and each girl that resided within the home.

My room was the closest room to the House Mother's room. The other girls in the home had their room at the opposite end of the house. I had the room to myself because I was the most outspoken and had A LOT of baggage.

I was moody and withdrawn at first. I would have fits of nightmares in my sleep and Mom Shirley would observe me and record the dreams while I slept and played them back to me when we had our one-on-one sessions. In these dreams, I would lash out physically, fighting the air, kicking and screaming at the top of my lungs, cursing and crying. I would often wake myself up when I would scream and cry my eyes out in the arms of Mom Shirley when she entered my room to console me.

When she would replay these tapes in our closed sessions, I would be absolutely startled at the words I used and the sounds of terror and despair that came to me in the night while I slept.

These repressed memories that haunted my dreams were ones of abuse and neglect at the hands of others.

Shirley would speak softly and lovingly to me. She would approach the dreams in a manner that helped me to relax and open up to her. I would receive more hugs from Shirley in the time that I resided in this home than I had ever gotten. She often told me she loved me, which is also a phrase that had failed to come out of my own mother's mouth. I felt safe with this nurturing woman and I was fulfilled by her presence and care. I truly believe Shirley was the first person whom I actually felt genuine love from who didn't condemn me or look down on me for being who I was.

My opening up in group, even if was just a little each time, would bring me closer to the other girls in the home and also begin the healing process in baby steps. This was very hard for me to let anyone in because it made me vulnerable to each person in that home and my walls were a hundred feet tall.

My new desire was to never leave this safe haven, my true home, and the people that I had learned to trust more than anyone in my life. Why would anyone ever want to leave that?

A few more months passed and I had been weaned from the care of the two House Mothers that resided in my first home. I had such reservations about moving on to the next level, yet I was a stronger person then, and I transitioned with hesitancy.

This second home housed the same amount of girls, some in which I had already known from the previous home and some new girls that had transitioned from another starter home. I opened up a little easier with these House Mothers and the girls at this house and friendships were made quickly. I was doing very well with group therapy. Even my one-on-one sessions were more comfortable to establish and my next step of healing was progressing well. Within three months, I transitioned to the third and final home.

This house was much different than the rest of the homes. It held tension and competition between the other five girls and myself. We had the same responsibilities but were given more duties, such as cooking on a certain day assigned to each girl. My walls that I worked so hard to break down just a few feet had risen a bit and I did not trust anyone as I knew none of these girls.

These girls had a much stronger personality than I had known at the previous houses and that made me uncomfortable and I was moved into a room that held four girls, including myself, instead of the double occupancy room I had come from with the second home that I lived in.

We were also given the opportunity to go to an outside public school, which also meant drug testing. I was nervous about attending school but I knew it was the next step to "graduating" and going home to our family.

Two days before my first day of public high school, I decided that I needed a tan. I laid down on the picnic table behind our home and proceeded to rub Crisco oil all over my body. It was a warm day with a decent breeze and not too long after I had flipped over, I fell asleep not shortly after I had settled into place on my back to sunbathe.

When I woke up about an hour and a half later, my body was on fire. I went inside the home and the House Mother reached up, put her hand to her mouth, and immediately rushed to my side. She pushed me towards the bathroom to view myself and get me into a cool bath with vinegar to help diminish the stinging pain of my horrendous sunburn. This was not your ordinary sunburn; this was a second degree burn that went from my forehead all the way down to my feet. Even my eyelids had blistered!

The next two days were excruciating for me and I could barely walk, sit, or bathe. My eyelids were filled with serous fluid and the blisters kept me from being able to completely open my eyes. I was drenched in lotions and homeopathic remedies to aid in my recovery, but nothing truly helped and the saddest part of it all was that I was not given the reprieve of missing the first few days of public school to recover and look more like a normal human being.

So, off to school I went with a cute figure, platinum blonde hair from the summer days, and all I could wear was extremely loose-fitting clothes and zero make up. I was so embarrassed and shy, not letting anyone approach me and I hid as well as I could behind my new school books. After a week had passed, my skin had gradually taken on healing and major peeling. I looked like a red breasted robin molting layers of skin, which would fly off me if the wind blew even mildly.

A few weeks into this new school, my skin had healed and I looked better. I was able to wear clothing that fit better and accented my cute figure and make up was easily applied without any pain. I cannot remember making friends but I didn't think I had any enemies.

What I do remember, was my first outside, part-time job given to me from the facility that I belonged to. I was employed at a large nursery that worked with and guided developmentally disabled teens and adults. What an amazing journey this employment gave me! I loved every moment I spent at this job of mine. I felt blessed, renewed, and important!

My self-esteem rose to a level I had never known existed. I felt complete here with these wonderful people and the counselors that ran the nursery. I remained at this job during the rest of the school year.

As the following summer came, I was bored. There was no longer a part-time job. I became frustrated and out of sorts. My moods had changed and I became bitchy. I needed the challenge of school and I missed my position at the nursery. I was regressing slowly into a shit starter and a sexual deviate. I would often sleep with Stephanie, a lovely robust and very beautiful Hispanic girl.

I was very easily influenced by the other girls who held stronger, more antagonizing behaviors. One of the girls had snuck in alcohol and we all partook in the elixir to establish a cool buzz that we used to know and enjoy.

The next drug snuck in was marijuana. Once a month, our House Mother would take all of us to an outside venue to eat or listen to music in the park not too far away from our home. We met a group of boys that did not live too far from where we resided.

The girls and I obtained their address and I was the idiot that chose to abduct our house station wagon and drive over to these boys' home to party like rock stars. I had beautiful long nails and was pretty striking at this time in my teen years. I remember being singled out by one of the most attractive boys to come along in my life since being employed at the auto shop. I also recall that I was so high that I literally watched, while in a haze, as my thumb nail burned slowly down to the tip of my finger.

Well, we know what comes after doing something we know is wrong— KARMA. One of the girls in the home who did not attend our little outing had found out from one of the girls that did attend, and I was ratted out.

I was given the opportunity to speak on my behalf and tell the house parent who had gone out with me, but I wasn't a rat. I was then sent to a beginner house once again to start over, made to leave outside school and attend classes on the campus with the newer inductees, and back to square one I went.

A new girl had entered our community, Tina, and we had soon fallen for one another. We passed letters through the girls at the separate houses we resided in, snuck kisses behind trees when we knew we could get away with it and touched fingers when casually walking by one another at any given time.

Most of the other girls were infatuated with the idea of us having a love affair, as this was not just taboo, but desired by many just because it contained feelings that we all desire: just to be admired and cared for, no matter what the sexual orientation be. The soap opera was undeniably one to be watched and felt by all. This was completely unacceptable, as well as dysfunctional at the facility, ultimately giving me three strikes, ending my stay at the Group home for girls. Tina, having been relatively new to the facility, was terminated immediately.

Michele Desmond

It was then my time to leave the facility and all of the progress I had made. I was a failure and a loser in my mind's eye.

Pride House

Nearing the end of 1983, the courts then sent me to a drug rehab in Van Nuys, California. The counselors were good. I was once again getting straight A's. There was sex going on there and there were drugs. I was still a part of all the bad that belonged to this place but had also decided that I didn't want to feel the way I did anymore.

Pride House was a good place to be. School was challenging. We played many sports, were gifted with outings when our community was all doing well, and the therapy was intense. I was given different jobs within Pride House during my stay, but the one that stuck out the most which I enjoyed more than any other was being the dishwasher. I worked with industrial sized sinks, large sanitizers and steamers, and I had the place to myself. It was the only time I was allowed to be alone and I was happy about that.

During my life in recovery, it seemed there was always someone there, in my space, near me, telling me what to do and how to feel. At Pride House, it was different. We were given chores, left alone to

57

make friends, and given challenging work to do in therapy and in our school classes.

Our therapy consisted of working on handbooks, telling our stories, answering questions about our family life and upbringing, and general "get to know you questions." I loved school time. I wish the classes would have lasted longer and that I was given harder work to do. My favorite subject was Creative Writing and I truly excelled at it.

I began opening up more in depth to the counselors as to what had happened to me when I was young. Group therapy was difficult at first. We had to speak to an empty chair while picturing the people who hurt us and talk to the chair about how we felt regarding what they had done to us. This was so difficult for me and I resisted at first, but then I couldn't hold it in any longer. I let it all out and I was quite descriptive about every evil deed that had been done to me.

I had still compartmentalized most of my sexual abuse and did not speak of the pornography tapes or encounters in Hollywood and Beverly Hills. I was too embarrassed to speak of these matters openly at this time in my life. It sickened me to think that I was a part of such distasteful occurrences.

About six months into my being at Pride House and having gained the trust of my counselors, I was asked by UCLA to be a part of a panel with the subject being, "Drug Abuse and Suicidal Tendencies," to 3rd and 4th year students attending UCLA to get their Psychology Degrees. I was nervous to do so but I was also thrilled that I was asked, out of over 60 other kids in our community, to complete this task.

When the day arrived to complete this amazing opportunity, I, along with my counselor, traveled to UCLA and went into this immense college/city where I felt immediately intimidated.

The classroom was enormous! The seats looked just like I had seen in the movies. Floor seats, cascading up towards the ceiling, and every seat in the house was taken. At first, I could not breathe and my heart began to race. I felt flush and became nauseous. My counselor noticed this and talked my anxiety down with breathing exercises and a cool glass of water.

It was the most astounding event I had ever attended. There were four of us on that panel, the other three I didn't know were from other rehabilitation facilities.

The professor began by asking us to introduce ourselves and stating what facility we were residing at. We made our introductions and then the questions began to fly towards us!

We were asked the typical questions: When and why did we start taking drugs? What type of childhood had we grown up in? Was there physical or sexual abuse of any nature while growing up? Did we experience any type of neglect?

I said yes to all the questions asked, so that made me the one that was asked the most questions! I held strong to my emotions most of the session yet had to release a few tears when I opened up about my own personal abuse. I actually noticed many students attending that event tearing up or even crying when I told my story.

The most memorable part of the event that sticks in my mind is when I was asked about my attempting suicide and how can others be helped to alleviate the pain that draws one near to yearning for their life to end.

I remember telling these students that it is not THEIR fault if their patient follows through with ending their existence, that they had done the best that they could do. If they held themselves accountable, they would never continue to practice.

I stated, "It will happen. Death happens. People give up because the pain is too severe and when a person is broken beyond repair, then the pieces cannot be put back together and the shattered life feels the need to leave because that is the only peace they will ever know." I then began to cry as my own pain rose and I noticed more tears on some of the students I was nearest to.

A few weeks after attending the UCLA conference, I was mailed a letter from the college thanking me for my participation and my candid display of the desire to inform others on the field that they were working on. I can't recall how I felt exactly, but I do think that I had been acknowledged, respected, HEARD, and validated. This was the beginning of a very positive and therapeutic way to heal and continue gaining control over my mental health.

I continued to make strides at this facility and then fell short when a very attractive boy came to reside with our community. His name was Butch. He was a tough ass, good looking, and I could not keep my hormones at bay nor my explicit thoughts of all the things I would enjoy doing with him if I ever had the chance. Eventually, I had the chance.

I knew that there were others in Pride House that were involved in "affairs" but we kept a pretty good tight-lip on this as we did not wish to get caught, of course. But, as all good things eventually come to an end, these hidden relationships soon came out.

The kids that came clean were me and a couple of other kids. This drug rehabilitation center did not, under any circumstances, make us wear our clothes inside out or shave our heads. We were dealt with "in house" and reprimanded to extra chores, no outings of any sort, extra time in our rooms, etc. If there was a repeat offender with two strikes, then they were let go from the facility and we never saw them again.

This was my first strike.

My counselor stated that it was a hiccup and that he believed in me. No one, and I mean no one, had ever said those words to me in that context: straightforward and to the point. It was so good to hear.

My counselor thought it was time for a meeting with my mother to tell her of what I had gone through as a child. I wasn't ready for this. I went ahead with it and when I talked to my mom in front of my counselor, she said it was all in my head! I was going a blow a gasket, I knew it was coming but I didn't know when.

After a time of being on restriction from certain activities, I was able to resume my regular classes, attend all outings, and went back to my regular chores.

I loved school. I really did. I was challenged and my creative writing was excelling. My school teacher stated that someday I should become a writer; that she could "feel" my words. She said that they were not just words, they reached the person reading, they captured the attention of the audience perusing through my stories, the reader was immersed in the story and walked my journey with me. She stated to me that I had some very beautiful and heartbreaking stories to tell that SHOULD be told.

While school was in session, I was told to visit with my counselor and teacher in a brief meeting. I was told that my school work for graduating was complete but that I needed to keep attending as there was nothing else for them to do with me and I would not receive my diploma until I had officially left the program and Pride House. I did not take this lightly. I felt I had put in my time. I reacted poorly and ran away to pout and rebel. NOT GOOD. This is where I blew my gasket.

I made the tremendous mistake of leaving the best place that could have helped me and walked out the front door, towards the closest on ramp, headed back to Orange County. I walked down Van Nuys Boulevard and I hitched a ride with a truck driver.

Right now, my chest is clenching up and my stomach is tied in knots. These next few paragraphs are not easy for me to write about. As the truck entered the Orange County district, the truck driver offered to make me lunch at his house before proceeding on into the area in which I lived. I did not feel comfortable with this but went along with it against my better judgment. As we exited the truck, my mind told me to run. However, I didn't because in some stupid way I felt as if I should trust this man and having lunch was not a bad idea because I was hungry.

We entered his home and he offered me a sandwich which I accepted. After lunch finished, the truck driver wanted to have sex. My mind was reeling. I knew what I should do was to just leave but the addict part of me stayed as he had offered me $400 to engage in sex with him, which I did. It was dirty and distasteful, and I felt filthy and nauseous afterwards.

I was given the $400 and he offered me a ride closer to my home. He lived in Garden Grove which was about 15 miles away from where I lived. I told him that I'd rather walk and proceeded down the road towards Santa Ana where my mother and sister still resided. After walking a long way, I cashed in one of the $20 bills, that the truck driver had given me, for bus money and rode the bus the rest of the way to Santa Ana.

When I had gotten closer to the area of my destination, I decided that I did not want to go straight to my mother's house. Instead, I walked to the home of my ex-girlfriend from high school. She wasn't home, however, her mother was and she gave me Pam's current phone number. I made the phone call and Pam said she was living in Corona with some roommates. I spoke with her for a bit and she drove out on her motorcycle to get me and take me back to her house.

I hopped on the back of her crotch rocket and at that time, there was no helmet law. It was approximately 45 minutes from Santa Ana to Corona and I froze my ass off. No helmet, no jacket, no fun!

When we finally arrived at her residence, there was a party going on. I had to run to the bathroom first and brush out all the knots in my hair. I looked atrocious. I was handed a beer upon exiting the restroom and the party was off to a great start. I was celebrating my short time of freedom.

The next 24 hours were a blur for me. I got pretty loaded and drunk and my ex-girlfriend and I spent some time together intimately. A day later, my conscience was tugging at me to go back to Pride House and deal with what lay ahead. I wasn't sure if I was going to be punished again or kicked out and that worried me.

When I arrived back at the facility, my counselor and I had a really long talk. I did not speak of the acts committed while I was away but I did tell him that I partied. I told him that I had felt bad for what I had done. I conveyed my true feelings on how I was stupid and irresponsible and I asked for another chance.

Indeed, that was the second strike and my probation officer came to pick me up to take me back to juvenile hall. I returned to court to see the judge. Having been just a few months shy of 18 years old, the judge set me free, and I returned to my mother's house. She actually let me come back and set rules for me to abide by, which I did for a short time.

I took the state proficiency test and scored in the top 15th percentile of the United States, received my diploma, and felt that I could begin a new life without all the dysfunctional behavior. I went for a job interview and was hired to be a clerk at a women's fashion boutique. I was so excited!! I could see a small light at the end of the tunnel!!

That evening, I called my old friend, Carol, to tell her of the good news. She seemed inadvertently delighted for me. We hung out, smoked some pot, and were chatting away... A car drives up and a friend of Carol's was driving. This was a classic car: a Volvo, vintage style. It reminded me of an old Chevy with round back, huge back seat, and ran like a top. It was very cool! We were offered to get in to ride around for a bit.

This guy, I can't remember his name, says, "Michele, remember when I said that I was going to kidnap you one day?" I said, "Yes." I remembered that he had, but I never paid attention to him because I never even thought I would see him again. He said, "Tonight is the night." I told him that I had to start a new job in the morning and I felt frantic but thought that Carol and I would be home by the end of the evening... I didn't take this guy seriously.

He drove far away from my home. I didn't even know where I was. I drank a concoction that he had made up for Carol and me and I began to feel very strange. Little did I know... he had put liquid acid into this drink he had given to me! I was flying like crazy by the time we reached our destination.

We exited the car and I said to Carol that we had to be back by midnight so I could work in the morning. She said not to worry about it, that she would make sure we got home okay.

I'm tripping out and Carol's tripping out and the guy that drove is laughing his ass off at us! He walked us into this studio apartment where this guy was giving tattoos. This studio was dingy and smelly, dirty, and claustrophobic to me. I could hear noises from underneath the apartment. Someone was yelling and knocking right underneath the floor! I said out loud to Carol, "What the hell is that?" The guy giving the tattoos, his name was Rick, says, "Oh, it's just my wife!" I was like, "What the hell?" Rick stated that his wife was tweaking under the house. I was mortified! I didn't even know what "tweaking" meant!

This noise continues under the apartment and Rick goes outside and starts yelling at his wife to knock her shit off. I'm confused and on an acid trip from hell, wondering where I was and how I was going to get home. Carol is laughing her ass off, I can't locate the guy who drove us to this unknown location, and I am now scared shitless!

On this evening, I was introduced to the drug methamphetamine. Time and space were gone. This drug caught hold of me and did not let go for several years. I did not return home to a new and better life. I was, once again, LOST. I was introduced to the needle and that's how I began using my drugs.

The day after we arrived in this town that I hadn't even asked where we were, I was getting my first tattoo of a unicorn. I had to jump up several times to throw up due to the pain of the needle and coming down off of all the drugs I had ingested.. The tattoo was stunning. This guy, Rick, was an amazing artist. Later I found out that he was an escaped convict... he had killed a cop and was hiding out... *What the hell?*

I had adjusted, or so I thought, to being high all the time. The days went by like hours. This meth was keeping me up three and four days at a time. I finally learned the name of the town I was in— Lake Elsinore. A month or so goes by and we are all still doing cocaine, meth, and smoking pot.

A gal, name forgotten, had some good drugs and I began working for her, doing various chores for my drugs. This was the type of life I had chosen to stay in on a daily basis: to get high and fade out of reality. Looking back on this, I can't explain why I stayed. And I cannot tell you how a person would remain in such a life after all these disgusting acts and behavior remained. I was neck deep in hell and could not think like a normal human being.

I look back now and see how sick I was. I figured I would die from an overdose and that would be that. I never thought that I would make it to the age I am now and live to talk about such things.

Rick was giving tattoos to a lot of people. One night, a buddy of Rick's, named Roger, came to have a tattoo of a mushroom put on the back of his calf. Roger was gorgeous! Long brown hair, Native American, and beautiful. I fell hard for the guy. I was no longer entranced with Rick and he was pretty tired of me. I'd become so immersed in the meth and I was no longer sane.

I left Rick and was homeless for a couple weeks, so I lived in my neighbor's dog house in their backyard. I shit you not. This dog house was my home for two weeks. I stayed out and about during the day and when it got dark, I climbed into the doghouse and that is where I slept. I lived on flour tortillas, peanut butter, and water from the hose in the yard. I was filthy. I'm sure I stunk to high hell and I was so high that I didn't even care! How sick is that?

This neighbor eventually took me in. He was also a drug dealer and I traded sex for a place to live. This was a party house like no other. I did drugs that I never knew existed. I then began seeing Roger who I had met at Rick's house. Roger was married but separated from his wife. She lived in the studio next to Rick's place which was just a few doors down from the new place I was staying. Terry was her name, and she knew I was seeing her husband. I was 18 and Roger was 25.

Terry saw me standing on the balcony of this place I was hanging out at and she called me out saying she was going to kick my ass. I thought I was tough shit so I went downstairs to have it out with her. It was pretty brutal: a little bit cat fighting and a lot of punches. I didn't think this would happen but I won the fight. I walked away like I was some sort of bad ass. I was never bothered again by Terry and eventually moved in with Roger. We had a dog named Bubba and a Golden Pheasant named Pete. We also had some turkeys. Roger was cool. He was my first love. We were together three years and it was completely dysfunctional. Sex and rock'n'roll man. That's all it was. That's where I was introduced to heroine. We snorted it, we smoked it, and then we shot it. I became pregnant with Roger's son, cleaned up immediately, and then we miscarried at six months.

Roger and I split up a couple times and I went back to living with my mom. I got a job as a security guard for the Orange County Register. I looked pretty spiffy in my uniform and felt good that I was contributing to society. I was still doing meth and also selling it but I was maintaining my job and life.

I worked swing shift at the newspaper factory. One evening after work, I drove over to a friend's house to party. I was still wearing my security uniform and upon knocking hard on the door, pressed my way in to give everyone a scare as a cop. They did not take this well for a few seconds and I saw a gun come out from someone's side. No one was shot but I was severely reprimanded about the hoax I had just played.

The night of partying ensued and a guy that I had seen a few times at my friend's home had just shot up quite a large dose of cocaine. He immediately went in to a seizure and everyone started freaking out not knowing what to do!

I have no idea how I knew this, but someone went to put their finger in this guy's mouth to keep the guy from swallowing his tongue. I yelled out to stop and grabbed the spoon this guy had just used to shoot up with and put it in his mouth to keep his tongue level. Needless to say, the guy bit down so hard on the spoon that he broke his two front teeth but he lived! The craziest thing about it all, was when he came out of the seizure, he immediately wanted to do another bump and we all exclaimed, "NO!" His girlfriend drove him home after gathering themselves briefly. I left shortly after that myself.

Looking back on this, I am floored at myself for being so immersed in such a trashed life and that I am still breathing to this day!

My dealer at the time, whom I had met through Roger, was one of the biggest in Lake Elsinore. Dude had eight kids and I fell hard for one of them, Donnie.

I was still working and seeing Donnie. I eventually quit working, kept dealing drugs, and moved in with Donnie. Our home was great. Ha!

We lived in a cab over camper which sat on saw horses in between a hog pen and a chicken coop. We had no running water and used propane for heat and cooking. We had to go inside the mobile home where his parent's lived to shower and go to the bathroom.

This mobile home housed Donnie's parents, Donnie's younger sibling, and was the meeting spot for hanging out with the family when we were all tweaking or eating food as a group. Even Donnie's parents did meth.

This mobile home was also the most disgusting format of a dwelling I have ever remembered being in. Even though everyone was high on meth, the place was never clean. You'd think someone besides myself would have had the energy to help clean up. I did what I could but the place would be trashed within hours afterwards so I eventually gave up trying to help.

There were roaches that lived peacefully among the family on the walls and crawled along the carpets.

The mobile sat on a septic tank so they did not flush their toilet paper down the commode, even after going number two, as I will safely call it. The flies that housed themselves in their bathroom were so thick and so loud that showering made me vomit from time to time. Donnie and I constructed a shower outlet which connected to the camper shell in which to hose off. We used the shower hose for hot days and heated pots of water to clean up when the nights were chilly. Cleanliness was not a high priority as with most druggies deep in their addiction. When we were out of drugs, we actually drove to our friend's home to adequately shower and shave.

This huge corner lot was filled with trash and meth heads. We only came out at night. We were like vampires but not seeking blood, we just wanted meth. Donnie's dad would get a big score and we would run his drugs for him.

One night, Dude had a brick of meth sitting on the dining room table. I'd never seen a brick of meth before and was fascinated. He also had stacks of money sitting near him. He was weighing the dope and counting the money.

Donnie's little sister, who was about six at that time, was running around the house playing with her cousins. At a moment's notice, the kids all ran up to the table where Dude was doing his weighing and the kids ran their hands along the table to sweep up this powder and licked their hands!

So now, the house was filled entirely with whacked out, tweaking CHILDREN, running around and when Dude sees what the children had done, he whipped out his pistol and fired into the ceiling of the mobile home and everyone scattered! Donnie and I took off in my car and stayed away so as not to get caught in the cross fire. The children did not sleep for two days.

This was how we lived on a day-to-day basis.

In late 1989, I found out that I was pregnant. I was scared shitless, overwhelmed, and full of joy all at the same time! I cleaned myself up and decided to carry my child to full term. I had taken blood tests at the local clinic to prove my pregnancy and make sure all the blood work was good.

I was left a message to call the doctor back immediately at my friend's home. When I returned the phone call, I was informed that my child had a gene that caused birth defects and that I needed to go to the hospital for more blood work. When the tests were completed I was informed that my baby would indeed have a birth defect called Gastroschisis. Gastroschisis is where the umbilical cord connected to the baby at the belly button is not covered by the stomach. My baby had a hole in his belly and would need surgery when he was born.

I was sent to Loma Linda University where I was seen by specialists for this defect. I had asked if the defect was caused by drug use and found that it was actually a genetic defect on his father's side and not because of early drug usage. Donnie's cousin had the same defect and was fine after surgery.

I was given the option from the specialists of aborting my child but stood my ground and said that I was going to carry my child to term.

My pregnancy progressed. I was clean and healthy but living in such squalor that my Mother spoke to me about going to live with her before my baby was born and I agreed that it was best for all of us.

I week later, in the late 7th month of my pregnancy, my mother drove to where we resided and I packed my belongings into her car and left that life that I had known. Thank God for my mother!!!

I returned home with my mom and never looked back at the life I had been living. Things were going to get better from here on in.

I gave birth to my son in August of 1990.

1990 – 1998

Raising my very own baby for the first time was a frightening experience! I had NO idea what I was doing. He was so fragile and I was his only solace, yet my mother was such a wonderful guide to helping keep my sanity and naivety at this new chapter in my life.

During this time, my mother and I were actually becoming friends for the first time in our life together. We remained dear friends until she passed away.

I carried my son around in a pillow for fear of breaking him. My mother would chastise me at times and I could never get it across to her that I hadn't a clue as to what I was doing. He had been in my womb for nine months with a huge birth defect and I was afraid that anything I might do would break him. I'm sure a lot of you can relate.

When I gave birth to him in late August of 90, I had a C-Section and I don't know if I had mentioned this to you yet, but it was the most painful recovery I have ever had to deal with thus far. I crawled on my hands and knees for nearly two weeks. Thank God my son was being taken good care of until his time of coming home so that I could recuperate. Standing tall was NOT an option. Crawling was most comfortable.

While my son was in NICU for two and a half weeks, I would visit him daily, which was nearly a three-hour drive. My mother would lend me her car to go to and from the hospital where I would visit with him and pump breast milk for when he came home and to keep lactating for him. His dad never went to visit him….

When Wayne came home, he had nearly three months of frozen breast milk for those times that I needed a break from the actual breast feeding, as I was very tender at times. It also helped for when I went out to Lake Elsinore to visit his dead-beat dad. It was a shame that he didn't partake in his own son's upbringing until his son turned nearly a year old. Donnie finally moved away from his meth addicted family and went back and forth to get his fix every weekend as he had finally landed a job as a security guard on graveyard shift. I was happy that my mother had allowed and encouraged Donnie to move in with us.

Donnie was attentive when our son started interacting and began to crawl. It was good to see them together. My mother had a strong bond with my son and it was a delight to watch them together. She made my life so much easier and taught me what I needed to know as I hadn't had a clue. Her gift to me was cloth diaper service for a year, which was somewhat of a hassle but also taught me how she took care of us and the strain it would sometimes take to wash the diapers by hand prior to putting them in the bin to be picked up.

My son began to crawl and speak at an early age. My mother spoke to me as she reminisced about how I had begun to speak early on as well and had spoken complete sentences by the time I was nearly a year old. I was walking at fourteen months and running at the age of sixteen months. I don't ever think I was able to let her know how much of a god-send she was for me during those years of housing us.

When Wayne was five months old, I started working part time at a gym's daycare and was allowed to take him with me so he could nurse and I never had to leave him. I was grateful for that. He and I would ride the bus to and from work and I was thankful that I was given a position where I could keep him by my side every day. I couldn't bear to be without him.

The children at the day care were often left with me being ill with colds and the flu. I could not believe that they would disregard the health and well-being of the other children, let alone my own son, to obtain those same illnesses. It was outrageous and I was concerned that my son would never be truly healthy because of it. He fared well, even through the illnesses, and it made me at ease that he was getting the proper antibodies from nursing and being around the sickness at my work to become stronger and immune to those types of strains.

When Wayne turned a year old, my sweet mother had made him a lemon cake with tart frosting for his birthday… he hated it and cried at his first bite! We all laughed, then felt bad about his dilemma on his first year of age. He received many gifts and we videotaped his birthday for years to come and let him see himself when he was an infant. I also spoke to him in the video to let him know what a blessing he was and showed him all of his toys, where he slept, which was with us of course, and tell him I loved him so much, and to thank him for saving my life from a world full of drugs and chaos. I was becoming domesticated and was a happy mother.

In 1991, Donnie and I were having difficulties in our relationship and since we were no longer together, nor living with each other, I decided to reconnect with an old boyfriend, John, that I met back when I was a teenager and hadn't really lost contact with him. I met him at a concert that he was playing at and then we went to dinner and back to my place. Mom was out on her own date that evening and not returning until the next day. John and I had sex that evening and while doing so, he reminded me of how he had lost his virginity to me but that he knew all kinds of tricks as the years had passed. I felt uncomfortable at first but, as you all know, sex became easier as it went along. The next morning, John left and we stayed in contact often.

During Wayne's birthday month, I had also learned that I was pregnant with another baby. When I found this out, I stressed because I didn't know if it had been Donnie's baby or John's. I called John up to let him know this and he had always kept a journal of his life, which I wish I would've done so as not to have been dealing with this book and the memories that have come along with it. John looked in his journal, gave me the exact date of our night together, and I felt relieved. However, Donnie was chastising me constantly about my supposed infidelity, even though he and I were no longer a couple.

I remember getting off the bus while a conflict ensued in front of the people that were in transit with us. I got off on the next stop and decided to walk the rest of the way home, contemplating whether John was telling the truth and what to do with this pregnancy. I went to a clinic not long after our fight and spoke about getting an abortion and to my surprise, as I went to have the procedure done, I had learned that I had pneumonia and would not be able to have the abortion. I am not sure whether these nurses were telling me the truth, but I never returned to the clinic, and I learned I was having another son, and I was elated! Donnie's mom had offered up a name for our second son, Justin Time, first and middle name. I don't know if she was kidding but her facial expression showed that she could've been quite serious about it. Who knows? I craved nearly a gallon of milk daily and quite a few meatball subs during my pregnancy!

The time came to give birth to our second son and Donnie was unwilling to go to the hospital with me. I'm assuming it was because he still did not believe that it was his baby I was bearing. He said to call when I was ready to push. It was a travesty that I was alone for the duration of my labor until the final hour when he decided to show up tipsy from drinking.

As I delivered our baby, Donnie had the look of complete disgust, refused to hold my hand while in labor, and as the crowning commenced and when cutting the cord and seeing the afterbirth emerge from my body, Donnie never looked at me the same as he used to. It was heart wrenching! Again, Donnie never came to visit us in the hospital for the two days we were there. My mother attended those days and brought me a delicate glass swan with a single rose and baby's breath as a gift to us. I never let my baby return to the nursery at the hospital and I was warned that I could possibly roll over and smother my son from both the nurses and my mother. I knew in my heart that it would never happen and was very adamant that absolutely no one was going to take him from me.

When I came home from the hospital in two days' time, Donnie refused to acknowledge Keith because he was born with a full head of brown hair and my oldest was born bald with a little blonde tuft in the back of his head. To this day, my youngest son never got to know his dad and I will explain as I go on in writing this.

My oldest was elated to have a little brother to hold and I delighted in taking photos of Wayne caring for his tiny brother. I felt my life was complete with both of my boys and I was no longer interested in having any other children. Living in Anaheim, California with my mother, we were so close to Disneyland that we would take the boys out to the cul-de-sac with our lawn chairs and watch the night light up with colorful rays to their delight and ours as well.

One evening, Donnie was so drunk that I chose to go inside with my youngest son and lay low as he was a verbally abusive man at those times. He came into the house and I receded to the bedroom to keep my space. Donnie bombarded into the bedroom, got into my face with our newest baby, and we began to yell at one another. Before I was able to set Keith in his crib, Donnie proceeded to shove me onto the bed where I landed on top of our son and it frightened me to the point of where I called 9-1-1 and he was taken to jail for domestic abuse.

Donnie was released the next day, angry of course, but never laid a hand on me again until later on into the relationship.

My youngest son was nearly five months old as I told Donnie that we needed to move far away from his drugged-out family and we decided to move to central Oregon where his older sister resided. That late November, we were packed and heading out of California, away from all the shit. I told Donnie it was our family and our kids or he could never be with us. He said he understood and we made it to Oregon in three days' time.

Winter in central Oregon was a nightmare! What money we had saved up was depleted as Keith had caught pneumonia and was in very bad shape. I almost thought we would lose him. I did all that I was instructed to do for my baby, especially the steaming in the shower to open up his lungs then to wrap him a blanket nice and tight and take him out into the chilly air. I did this night after night, day after day, and the treatments were working! I was so grateful that he got well, but it took a little time.

When Christmas and New Year's came closer, I had decided that since Donnie would never stick to a job because he had one excuse after another and then his urine tests kept coming back dirty, I finalized the end of our relationship. Donnie claimed that it was just pot that was in his system but I knew better.

February rolled around and I had decided that I was happy just having my two sons and went to get my tubes tied. As we drove 40 miles away to a town called Bend with Donnie's sister, who joined on the road trip, Donnie proceeded to get belligerent and we had words. I was in the back seat with my boys and Donnie whipped his hand out and busted open my lip. I really don't remember the argument that we had but the boys started crying and Donnie's sister was pissed beyond words! I entered the hospital alone and had the outpatient surgery which went well. The nurses had seen my lip, so I discussed with them what had happened and they were quite adamant about calling the cops on Donnie for his abuse. I stated that I was okay and we went home without any more issues. No apology came but I really didn't expect one, as Donnie was always in the right, or so he thought.

There was a friend, Mike, that Donnie had made through his sister's family and Mike had the connections that Donnie sought. Donnie and I stayed living in the same household, a single-wide mobile home, as roommates.

I went to work as a waitress at the only restaurant in the town. This was a very small rural area with two grocery stores and a bar. A Podunk town but there were many lakes and rivers nearby in which to camp and fish.

At noon every day, Donnie would swing by the restaurant for me to nurse Keith and pump during the evening when I had long shifts. When I would return home from work, Donnie would take all of my tips earned that day and head to the bar for the evening. He and I cohabitated in the same home until early April.

During my employment at the restaurant, I trained for nearly two weeks and was set out on the floor by myself afterwards. My first customer, Mark, was quite the jerk, as he ordered a plain salad with lemon and two rolls. I screwed up the order and forgot his rolls and he yelled at me in front of the other customers which sent me back to the kitchen to cry! Afterwards, I always got his order right as he was in our establishment daily for dinner. I hated him and always said, "Here comes the asshole!"

After about a month, Mark and I became friends. He had a dry sense of humor and was a smart ass more so than anyone I had ever met. I learned to take his personality with a grain of salt and learned that he was clean and sober, which to my surprise made it much easier to be friends. Later down the line, he and I became much closer, even though Donnie and I were cohabitating as roommates.

One evening, I decided it was time to take this closeness to a deeper level and actually pushed my Volvo, which was a damned heavy vehicle, out of our driveway while everyone was asleep and drove over to Mark's place. It was rather a mess and I had learned that he had a family that he was separated from. First red flag. He also had four kids and I was not wishing to raise any more children! Thank goodness that I had my tubes tied as, obviously, this man was very fertile!

Mark and I spent most of the evening together and when I arrived home, Donnie was sitting in the living room with the boys and proceeded to jump my shit about going out. He was so livid that he went to the kitchen and grabbed the largest knife we owned and headed towards me screaming that he was going to slit my throat. I leaped onto the couch towards my babies and grabbed them to head out of the house and Donnie proceeded after me. He kept screaming to put the boys down so he could kill me and I was not about to do that and have myself or my sons hurt. Yes, I went about things completely backwards in my behavior and should not have done that, but Donnie and I had been done since December and I needed companionship. I wish I could take it all back— the sneaking out part that is.

Donnie threw the knife out into the dark yard and told me to bring the boys in. When I set them down to talk with Donnie about my being out, he grabbed my neck and began to strangle me until I nearly passed out. The babies were screaming. I was coughing and I picked up the boys once again and went straight to the bedroom and locked ourselves in to stay as safe as a mobile home door would allow us to be.

The next day came and my neck was bruised so badly that I had to go to the second-hand shop and buy a few turtle necks to wear while working.

It was hell on earth for a good week until Donnie made the decision to move out to his sister's place not far from where I lived. He visited the boys every so often but word of mouth stated that he was out partying more so than ever with this Mike guy, who I would never let into my house, or life, for that matter. I just felt so strongly that something was wrong with this guy. Turns out, there were many things wrong with him!

First off, I found out that he was gay and had a mad crush on Donnie! I told Donnie about it and he neither denied or accepted what I was telling him. He completely dismissed the idea and I just let it go. I then found out, many years later, that this Mike guy had molested Donnie's nephew many times over which scarred that boy for life. I will say that I have heard Donnie's nephew is doing much better now, with a family of his own, which I am very grateful for. I don't know what became of Mike. Had he been sent to prison or even prosecuted for molesting my nephew? I never asked and felt that was out of line to even question as we were not really family but just my sons' cousin by blood.

My youngest son's birthday came in late May and we had a cool party for him. My mother and step dad drove up to give us furniture and visit for nearly a week. They stayed at an inn in town and we had a good time. My mother suggested that the boys and I return to California to live and I was too stubborn to say yes, which I still regret to this day. So many regrets.....

After my son's birthday, I allowed Mark to move in with me. He took very good care of the boys while I worked and the house was clean with dinner on the table when I arrived home. We all ate at the table as a family, which was something that Donnie and I never did, so that felt all right. He drew, colored, and painted with them showing me the art when I got home. He was teaching my oldest to read a little and to tie his shoes. I actually came to feel that this guy was my "Mr. Right."

Mark was clean and sober, fit, and so intelligent with a beautiful, deceitful smile that swept me off of my feet and I was enamored with his doting on me. He was a father of four kids that were well behaved as he was a strict father.

Mark came from a background of abuse himself. His father was a literal genius, having written several books and actually believed that it was righteous for him to be an abusive alcoholic, especially at dinner times when the family of six were all together for the show. Mark's mother was the center of the abuse and humiliated at every possible moment. The beatings were viewed by all of the children. Mark's dad made sure of it. Mark's father was a raging alcoholic and it seemed to run in the family as his two sisters and brother had the same issues but worked hard to conquer and break the chain.

I enjoyed his family and they accepted me and my two sons with open arms. Apparently, Mark's first wife was not well received and had no contact with the rest of Mark's family. I had heard opinions from all his family members and took to heart what I was getting myself into when I was to face her and be her kid's stepmother.

Mark was seriously into his recovery (or so I thought) and led weekly meetings at a coffee shop in town. We would all attend and I spoke about my addictions and problems, which helped me not feel so overwhelmed. I met a gal in the meeting and we became friends. After a few weeks, I had asked her to become my sponsor, which she gladly accepted. Later that evening, Mark come clean about the fact that he and this gal had been having an affair for quite some time prior to our getting together and that it would not be a good idea. I stopped going to those meetings after that.

I began to distance myself from Mark a bit over the fact that two married individuals, working on bettering their lives and those around them, would have an affair, which, to me, completely negated the term "recovery"—in my eyes anyways. I never asked Mark to stop going to meetings but he chose to do so and that's when things became bad which lasted nearly eight years.

Mark attempted to do his own recovery at home. He seemed to be doing well. He wasn't working much as a carpenter and I was supporting the household until he got back on his feet.

Mark had known about the strangulation from the evening spent with him. He did not confront Donnie about it and stayed calm when the two were around each other. I had spoken to Mark on many occasions about my life as a little girl, the abuse, and sheer madness of my life in general. He claimed he would never hurt me in anyway and I trusted him.

The following month, work had picked up at the restaurant and I came home a little later than usual on some nights. One evening, Donnie had the kids for the weekend, and I asked Mark if he wanted to go meet up with the other girls from the restaurant to play pool and video games at the tavern with me. He stated that I wasn't to leave the home and we were staying in for the night. All I did was work and live as a housewife. I hadn't been out in so long and I said that I was going to go out anyways and meet with the girls for a few hours.

Here is where the abuse begins…..

Apparently, Mark did not like that I had crossed what his rule for the evening was and decided to throw me down to the floor and put his hands around my neck. The insane thing about all of this is that he KNEW what a trigger that was for me and it made him smile as he choked me.

Now I should have kicked this jerk out of my home that very moment. I should have gone back to my mother's area of residence and picked my life up there. I never used to pay attention to what was best for me. I always paid attention to what I would lose if I did make a move.

SO…. this is what my mind chose to do. I weighed the pros and cons of Mark's behavior. He was so good with the boys and was intelligent and SOBER. He made a good living when the work was available and I could forgive him for this transgression. He said he would never hurt me again…………...*What the hell was I thinking?!!!*

When Donnie would come to pick up the kids, Mark would not let me talk to him. He said it was for my protection, yet now I realize that it was such a control mechanism that he was putting into effect and I could not see the forest through the trees.

Within a few months, Mark had spotted a place for sale and had convinced the owners to put the place in my name and I had become a homeowner without even knowing how it had happened. I never even attended the negotiation meeting. Mark brought the paperwork home and told me to sign them, which I did, naive and trusting that all would be well. It was on an acre of land loaded with Ponderosa pines and a three-bedroom double-wide trailer with an addition of a 16'x16' bedroom for a mere 20 grand. Mark even rigged it somehow that no down payment was necessary! I gotta tell you, in some areas of Mark's psyche, he was a brilliant man. Then there were the times that his brilliance became a nightmare as his controlling state was so erratic and abusive towards this family we had merged together.

Our first night at the place, we had all of our children with us and made it a slumber party in the large living room with the wood stove going. The electric hadn't even been turned on yet so we basically camped indoors for two days and assessed what we now had as an owned parcel of land and dwelling.

Mark's ex-wife played a good martyr, saying that Mark abused her as often as possible. She always made mention of how she was the perfect wife and never did anything wrong, yet her own kids would tell me of her infidelities and the drug usage that became a huge part of all of her kids' lives as they grew up after Mark and I divorced. I, still at times, miss them and the seven years we spent together. Every summer and most holidays were spent with our family of eight.

Altogether, I was a mother and stepmother to five boys and one girl. I had moments of being overwhelmed at times, of course, yet remember more good times than bad when it was just the kids and myself and Mark was away at work. I did notice how the moods changed when he would get home. The air would be thick with tension and the kids no longer laughed or smiled much, which I didn't understand and when I asked Mark about it, he just said that they knew their place when he was around. Mark would have them all stay outside until dinner time, saying that they didn't need to be in the house during the day and they had to knock on the door if they wanted to come inside for something. I didn't understand the manner in which he spoke to them. This man would give his kids a look and they would cower down so quickly it made me cringe. I made sure, when Mark was not home, to make their stay the best it could be and I know they genuinely loved me for that.

On our land, we made tepees, forts, played tag and hide and go seek. When we made our 70-mile round trip to the actual real town closest to us, I would take them to the craft store and we would buy feathers and felt to make head dresses for all of them. Mark's daughter and I would go do girly things together so that we could get our girl time in as she was quite shy at first but we became very close quickly and that made me happy. They really were great kids and my two sons loved them as well. I seriously did not mind being a mom to six kids!

When the kids would go back to their mother, it was, often times, a struggle to get them to come back to me emotionally. I'm guessing it was because of the manipulation and denial that they were actually allowed to be loved by another female in their lives. It was all a huge mind game between Mark and his ex-wife to mentally and emotionally abuse one another, which affected the kids more than these parents could ever imagine.

When it was just my sons with Mark and myself, I would take the boys to daycare and go to work with Mark. He was a good teacher and I learned the trade of framing and having been a roofer from my earlier years, I was able to bring a fair amount of my own knowledge to the table which was impressive enough to be put on the payroll with his company. I learned how to use all the tools of the trade and made a good partner in the trade that Mark had been into since he was eleven years old.

Although I never saw my checks, which I disliked, the bills were paid and we had a stocked fridge. Life was becoming good and I learned my place as an employee, mother, and future wife. Mark was molding me into who he wanted me to be and I conformed to that lifestyle, thinking that was how it was supposed to be. Mark had to always come before my kids and he was head of the household no matter how we felt about it.

There were times that we were not allowed to leave the dinner table until all of our plates were clean. This occurred mostly on the nights that Mark would have his meal of cow heart and Brussel sprouts, which he KNEW we all could not stomach well so we sat at the table until I would plead to him not to make us eat that meal anymore. He would scold us and then school us how we needed to learn about different foods and how this heart and those sprouts were good for our bodies and minds. We were made to eat that fucking meal once a month just to be subjected to his ridicule as he sat and scowled while my sons cried over the taste of this awful meal we were made to eat. If I would cross this man in front of my children, I was beaten that evening when they were in bed at the opposite end of the house.

The beatings began to become a cycle, about every three to four months at first. It was when the kids were with their dad, which was a rarity, or when they slept. Our bedroom was on the opposite side of the mobile home and I was often stifled or strangled as the beatings occurred and the sick part of it was that afterwards, Mark would stroke my hair and kiss my arms or neck or wherever he landed his fists or menacing grasps.

The sickest part of all of this is that I know now that I was being conditioned into his slave and he became my master. This was his world of BDSM and control that was so anti what the world of BDSM really was....to be safe, sane, and consensual. His conditioning was his way of molding me and manipulating me into accepting this as a way of life... which I eventually embraced.

LOVE, HATE, SEX... that became my reality and world with Mark. Mark was to be taken care of before my kids, doted on in public, and I was to let him have sex with me no matter where we were. I remember we had stopped for gas when we went into the city. Mark had the boys stay in the car and locked the doors at the gas pump while he made me go into this disgusting single bathroom attached to the outside of the station. This little room housed a filthy urinal, toilet, and sink. I was in the midst of grime, grease, and muck which permeated my nostrils and the odors of shit and piss made me gag! This is where the first occurrence of his humiliation came in a sexual manner outside of our home.

Mark truly became my master and I was his slave. He made me smile, laugh, and bleed. He brought such ecstasy into the relationship, combined with the aftercare of his beating me, and it became an addiction. Some of you will understand this and some of you will not.

Our "family" owned a nice van which had captain's chairs and a reclining seat in the rear of the van. Mark would take me to remote locations in the vast amount of woods we had in our area of central Oregon and make me have sex in the van, in the woods, or wherever he pleased. These ventures became an addiction for me as well. Not knowing where I was going, if I was going to be beaten that day or made love to with the utmost intensity, gave me the thrill of a lifetime! I couldn't wait to see what came the next day. It was a roller coaster of heaven and hell and I was hooked on being the victim or the princess... it became my drug of choice, all the while putting the rest of the family on the back burner until I was then allowed to actually be a mother and a housewife.

I want to state here that Mark was still maintaining his sobriety and I was happy that he was doing so, even though the shit got real bad at times. I could not even imagine what it would have been like had he not been sober. I later found out how horrific my/our lives were to become when he fell off the wagon………. And yet, I still stayed with him.

I was often reminded of how no one would love me like he did, how no one would want a single mother with two kids to take care of, and he would always be there for me but that I had to endure the rules of havoc and abuse to be loved and for my boys to have a roof over their heads.

I was not allowed to work unless it was with Mark. When he would take off on a binge away from home, I would get a job doing whatever I could. I would cut wood for neighbors, babysit, house keep, whatever I could to keep food on the table and a roof over my sons' heads.

I took a job at a local market and was a deli clerk. My self-esteem rose and the kids and I were actually doing better. Mark had been gone about five weeks and even though I was "jonesing" for my fix of sex and abuse, I was happy that I could actually breathe in my own home. I could see the relief in my boys' eyes and feel their love coming back for me. My paychecks were small but adequate until it was nearing winter and our bills were stacking up.

I remember after the beatings and the romance returning during our "cycles" that I would consistently go to the cop shop in Bend after being beaten and Mark taken to jail to claim that it was all my fault and that I had started the wars so as to have the charges dropped and then Mark would come home only to kill what I had been trying to accomplish as a good mother that just went down the toilet every time I took that fucker back.

Deschutes County, Oregon, back in the day, of course, which was 1993–1996, was not a place for the police to actually keep abusers in jail and to accept that the victims were actually the pawns and nothing was done to be of use to anyone other than the abuser.

My life was a fucking mess. There was this cycle of ultimate heaven in my eyes. My fiancé was a very loving, passionate man, a good step dad to be, and of such high intelligence and vast manipulation that I absorbed and became that type of person entirely. Mark came first, the kids came second, and I was a piece of shit. I did not understand that life was actually not supposed to be that way! I was not allowed to have friends, except in our church where we attended but I was not allowed to visit with anyone alone or be a part of any of the women's groups.

I pleaded with Mark for us to go to counseling. Mark agreed and said it would take place with our pastor and he, Mark, would lead the session and I was only allowed to speak of things he thought that I was doing wrong. I would be beaten if I muttered anything that I was told not to and I learned my lesson after attempting to do so and had to miss Wednesday worship with our family and the church because I had noticeable bruises that were not to be seen.

After a few months of meeting with our pastor, I was approached by the pastor's wife and she said that I should leave the relationship. I wish I would have listened.

One day, I took my boys to the "big city" of Bend, Oregon, to apply for food stamps and any other aid that I was able to get to survive. There were pamphlets in the office regarding domestic abuse and I grabbed one to read when we returned home.

Here are just a few recollections of abuse that I would like to talk about.....

I recall several times where Mark had gone out to drink and then come home and beat my ass. My oldest, Wayne, had literally jumped onto Mark's back screaming at him to not hurt his mother and Mark would just laugh in his face. *What the hell had I done to my child?* I had no idea of the scars that my decisions and behaviors would be lifelong for my boys... another regret.

There was a day when Mark came to the house to abuse my sons and me by removing the washer and dryer from the home. I had to wash and rinse my family's clothes in the bath tub, then hang them to dry on the clothes line out back. When Mark could see that I was learning to work through the troubles he brought, he then cut the clothesline so I had to hang our clothes around the house to dry.

Another time, Mark decided to remove our heat source from our home. He removed the wood stove. The mobile home had a furnace, but this was not adequate enough to heat our home and we all hovered underneath piles of blankets next to the furnace vents in the house just to keep warm!

Mark had taken a wood splitting maul to the counter tops in the kitchen so I would not have space to prepare food for my sons. These acts were done deliberately in front of all of us so that Mark could soak in the power he had over this family and to mentally scar us.

One evening, the boys were in bed, I was watching television and I had heard a noise out around the side of our home. I knew it was Mark! I picked up the phone to dial 9-1-1 and the phone line had been cut! I went to gather the boys up from their slumber and took them out to the car to get away from the area and my car hood was up! I put the boys in the car, had them lock the doors, and looked under the hood. All of the spark plug wires and distributor cap had been removed so I was going NOWHERE! I quickly gathered the boys and we ran to the nearest neighbor's home to call the police.

When the officers arrived, they looked at all that had been done to the phone line and my car, made a search of the property, and found Mark laying down under some bushes. They hauled his ass off to jail and, this time, I did not retract my statement of abuse.

Mark spent some time in jail, was not allowed back onto the property, and went to live in a motor home on the property of a family that belonged to our church.

After taking a few phone calls from my "friend" Debbie, who Mark was staying with, I decided to attend dinner at their place. Do not ask me why for I do not understand my thought process at the time.

I was lonely, afraid of doing all of this on my own, overwhelmed, and my addiction was still hovering.

Mark was cordial, polite, and seemingly working on himself. He led me to believe that he was doing counseling and wanted our family back together. I should have been smarter than that. I should have been stronger. I should have said no to getting back together with him.

Mark stated that he was moving to the Portland, Oregon area where he would continue his counseling, find work, and secure housing for all of us. I stayed in our home in La Pine with the boys, contemplating all that Mark had said, and resumed my life, while wondering if this man was going to follow through with all that he had promised.

Mark had indeed done what he had said in regard to housing and a good paying job. I had a live-in roommate who stayed with my sons while I traveled over the Santiam Pass to visit this new place and see if Mark was on the up and up.

To my surprise, he had indeed established a nice apartment in Tigard, Oregon. He had furnished it and set up a nice bedroom for the boys. It was close to all of the things that we needed and I would be allowed to go back to work. Wayne was getting ready to start Kindergarten and the school bus came right up to the apartments for transporting my guy back and forth. It seemed too good to be true!

So, I returned home, packed up the boys, regardless of asking their feelings on the matter, and headed out to Tigard to try this insane act of being a family once again.

Things were going so well at the beginning. I really felt like Mark was changing and that I would someday have that picket fence. We were both working separate jobs, had separate paychecks, and the boys were actually happy!

One Friday evening, Mark took his crew out for dinner and drinks. Mark came home drunk and the abuse commenced once again.

The fight was in front of my boys and as they huddle together on the couch in the living room, Mark upended the glass coffee table and it smashed to bits all over the carpet. I screamed for Mark to leave and he did, leaving me to clean up the mess and tell the boys I was so sorry ONCE AGAIN.

Mark came home a few days later, laid ten thousand dollars out on the couch and said that everything was going to get better, he promised. He became the man that we all loved and admired and the cycle continued all over.

Things were going well again for a few months and then the abusive language came, which I knew would bring about the physical abuse.

The boys were playing in their room, Mark and I were debating about something I don't recall, and words began to take on a new meaning.

Now, knowing that I was going to be hit at some point, I decided I would fight back this time. I had had it! The words that came from my husband's mouth took me to a dark place and I saw RED.

Mark, having been my best friend when we first got together, I had told him of all that had happened to me. He knew my soft spots, the ones that scarred me for life. And then he used them against me. He called me "Daddy's little girl."

So, this is where I then became the abuser. I had a lit cigarette in my hand and when I heard those words, I put that cigarette out in his ear. I then proceeded to punch and kick him in the ribs and blackened his eye.

Mark called the cops and I was taken to jail. The officer let me take the boys to our neighbor to stay with her while I went to jail. The officer looked up Mark's priors on him and decided to let me go back home that evening instead of keeping me overnight to see the judge the following day. He booked me and gave me my court date and drove me back to get the apartments we lived in and I stayed with the boys at my neighbor's place on the couch that evening.

Mark was away for the next few weeks and I changed the locks and went to court. Standing in front of the judge, feeling ashamed for my actions, I was told by this female judge that she had taken note of Mark's priors and was dropping the charges against me. I looked at her with my jaw wide open and didn't know what to say. The judge told me that it was time to leave the relationship and I said that I would do just that.

I went home, packed the kids up, and we drove down to California to live with my mother and step father until I could get back on my feet.

My mom and I enrolled the boys in school and I went to work for a temp agency where I landed a full-time job for a Honda Dealership. I was so happy! I then saved enough money and went to look at apartments close to my mother. I put a deposit down on my very own apartment for my kids and me. I was so proud!! We were to move in at the beginning of the following month.

A few days later, a visitor arrived at my mother's house while I was at work.....

In 1999, Mark came to California to gather me and the boys up again.

I wish my mother had never told me he had arrived, but she felt it was my right to know and to make the decision she hoped I would make, which was to stay in California and tell Mark to go to hell. Unfortunately, I was swept off my feet once again, by a man I adored, worshiped, and hated all at the same time.

Wayne did not want to leave with Mark and me. Keith was too small to have any say in the matter. So the three of us packed our things and drove off with Wayne staying behind in my mother's arms. I had abandoned him once again and hated myself for it. I knew he was in better hands than I could provide but that I would have him back in time when my marriage was mended and our family life intact. *Who was I kidding?*

April of 1999 was when we headed north up to Washington State. Crossing over the border of Oregon and into Washington, we came to the first town called Vancouver and decided to settle there.

We found a dingy old three-bedroom house that tilted to one side, smelled musty, and was not conducive to my happiness. Mark quickly found work and began framing for our landlord. Keith went to school just two blocks down the street and I was thankful for that because I had absolutely no idea where the hell we were and if the neighborhood we lived in was safe. I enjoyed walking every day to drop off and pick up Keith from school. We would then meander around our new neighborhood to check out the surroundings. What a shit hole of a town I had thought this was. The grocery store was filthy and the laundromat even worse. Mark couldn't have picked a worse spot for us to settle in.

Mark decided to plant a garden and we had a great time doing so. I had found out several weeks later that in between every tomato plant was a marijuana plant and I freaked out. There were a total of 14 plants that could have taken my son from me, landed me in prison, and all for the glory of Mark getting stoned all day long.

Just after six weeks of living together once again, I had found that even looking at Mark made me throw up, literally. One evening, I was soaking in the tub, Mark walked in and stated that I was seriously losing weight, which he found to be great, for him, of course, but he didn't realize it was because I could no longer live like I was and I couldn't hold down food any longer. I was literally throwing up because of the decisions I had made to leave my family and move back to a marriage that would never ever work.

I began scouting for jobs to help me gain money to leave Mark once again. Having done so, I saved every penny and in June of 1999, I moved across town to my own apartment with Keith and became empowered with the strength that I did not know existed.

I knew I had to do this on my own, without the help of my mother, who had been there for me so many times, in order for me to gain the power of MYSELF and carry on as a better mother for my sons.

I looked for a better paying job while Keith was in daycare. I became a temp at a mortgage company and did very well. I was still in search of a job that paid better and landed myself at a large company supplying cable television to customers all over Clark County and even Portland, Oregon. I didn't know the area and quickly taught myself the various routes and neighborhood after work so that I could be an asset to the company rather than a hindrance. I went to train for the job and had a blast, learning about amperage, carrying a 90-pound ladder properly, and to gaff a telephone pole to provide services to customers... I did very well at this job and made the most money I had ever earned my first year there.

At the end of August, I had put forth the effort to go to counseling, get Keith established in his new school, and secure a healthy environment for both my boys and me. I called my mother to let her know how I was doing on a weekly basis and when we both felt it was a good time to bring my son Wayne home, we did so. I was so happy to have him back. My family was complete. I worked very hard to give them both a stable home, which I had never done before. I saw Wayne and Keith smile every day and that made my heart happy. I was a good mom at last.

To even make things better for both of my sons, I would take one son out on a Friday, away from school, and we would do whatever he wanted that day. It was our special time together. The following Friday, I would do just the same for my other son.

My one-bedroom apartment and my new job were a great start to a new life with my sons. A few months into my new position as a cable installer, I was given a raise, and able to afford my own 3-bedroom house with a fenced back yard. My husband and I were finalizing our divorce and I made my way over to his place one day, snuck into the bedroom window, and stole my dog back, who I was not allowed to have at my apartment. This completed my happy home. Coco was an amazing little 4-pound pocket poodle. She was happy to be back home with us as well.

Our home was a happy one for a time. The boys started out at a new school and both seemed happy. I found a great baby sitter just across the street from their school, who had her own kids that all got along and I felt like my life was finally going to be all right.

In February of 2000, my divorce became finalized and my ex thought it would be cute to bring his new girlfriend to the courthouse to sign the documents. I was fine with that, especially when the authorities arrived to place the cuffs on him for his spousal abuse on ONE of several warrants that were out on him in various states and counties in which we had lived over the past 8 years. All our moving around had finally caught up with him. I didn't even know they were going to show up but knew someone must have been on my side that day. Needless to say, his girlfriend wasn't too happy about that and attempted to start a fight with me. I laughed nervously and the cops told her to back off.

I went back to work that day with a huge smile on my face!!

A little over a month later, my ex plead guilty to domestic violence, received six months in jail, and I never saw him again. I did try to regain contact with my four step kids but was told that my ex said if they had any contact with me, then he would write them all off. That was hard to take after being in their lives for so long.

My oldest son's birthday was coming up and my mother flew up to rent a house in Hood River, Oregon for a week. We had a great time playing in the water, putting our toes in the sand, and watching all of the wind surfers.

This was the first time I had heard the words "I'm very proud of you" come from my mother.

Time flew by too fast and I had to return to work, my mother flew back to California, and the kids were heading back to school soon as summer break was over.

Holidays with my children were never as great as my mother had set out to give to my sister and myself. I wasn't the best cook but we had a fun time making a mess in the kitchen that Thanksgiving.

My sons loved that they had their friends to hang with across the street as well as the buddies they had made across town at our first apartment in Vancouver.

Nearly a year later, settled into our home and doing well, I ventured out one evening to listen to karaoke at the nearby tavern. It was clean and I had friends that I worked with who went there occasionally, so I felt comfortable going alone. It was there that I met a man who would be a part of my life for the next chapter of what I hoped would be secure, happy, and healthy.

This man, Bill, was a great person who was sober, was secure in his career, and had a stable home. He played an important role in our family and the boys enjoyed his company and outgoing personality. We went camping, quadding, ice skating, skiing, and more... all the things that a family would do together.

Now.... this relationship was the most "normal" relationship...to date.

A year later, Bill proposed, I said yes, and then things got really weird.

My mother had given me a call and told me of her being abused by my step dad. Turns out, my mother had been abused off and on, in cycles, for the entire time she had been with Mike, my step dad. They had become a couple before Wayne was even born and this was the first I had heard of it! My mother was very good at keeping secrets.

I quickly spoke with my sister who was adamant about getting my mother out of the home and I said she should come and live with me. Mother never really confided in me about her abuse because she knew my own abusive marriage was hard on me but to know that my own Mother was being beaten would not go well with me, so this was all something rather new. She only confided this in my sister and no one told me anything.

I had found out that my mom had walked in on my step dad interacting on pornography sites online and she called him an adulterer. Her account to me then was what pushed me over the edge...... she stated that he literally picked her up and threw her out of the house, down six concrete steps, in her night gown, and locked her out of their home! She banged on the door to be let back in, sat on the steps for what seemed like forever, then walked across the street to her neighbors' house and slept on their couch until the early morning, when he walked over and took her back into the home, only to have Mike to beat her face in.

When my mother arrived at my home, her face was black and blue! I could barely even recognize her! We all know I have a temper and I had known of only one time that Mike had hurt my mother but that was a long time ago.. I had told my step dad that if he harmed my mom again, I would kill him..... but just having her with me and away from him was enough to spit in his face about. I should have given her more attention but I worked all the time. The kids were never home because they were either at school or with their friends. We rarely did anything as a family and I know she was lonely.... so lonely. I hold myself responsible for not being there more or her. She was always there for me..... always, no matter what, even when it became a strain on her own marriage, she was there.

I remember her sitting in the den, alone, gorging almonds, and sitting on her cell phone all the time. All of our bedrooms were upstairs and it hurt her to go up and down them so she stayed downstairs all day, on that one spot on the plush green sofa, and ate almonds......

Three months later she returned to my step dad.... I understand why. He was all she had that really gave her attention, even when it was totally dysfunctional, at least someone actually paid attention to her.

I didn't see it then, I was just pissed at her. Kids are so self-absorbed when they have their own lives, their own kids, and their own issues. Especially in a day like these days where the almighty dollar speaks volumes more than a simple hug or a drive in the country. Holding the cell phone instead of each other's hands is more important. Texting versus having a simple conversation while hearing one another voices.....it doesn't matter anymore to anyone. I was guilty of it myself. And I was also disgusted by it.

I know why she went back and she stayed there until her death. She said if she had to do it all over again, she would never have married him and never have returned to him after living in Washington, even with how lonely she was. I wish my eyes and heart would have been more open and more receptive to HER heart. Maybe she would have never left and we would have gotten a place of our own.

2001

Bill and I had constructed a two-story fort for the boys to play in and that housed bales of hay and bull's eyes for our compound bow practicing.

My birthday came around later that year and we had a small get together at the house: dinner, dancing, and a big butterfly cake to celebrate with. We had our neighbors, some co-workers, and a few friends of ours over that evening. As the evening died down, a few of my girlfriends and I began to clean up. My oldest son had his best friend staying the night and they helped out in the yard as well. When the party ended, friends went home and we went to bed, my oldest stayed up late with his buddy. My college and good friend, Mary had come to the party with her friend, Daniel, a nice-looking young marine and they were also staying the evening because they were drinking.

That evening, unbeknownst to me, Daniel had taken my son and his buddy up into the fort and gave the boys alcohol and attempted to engage in a sexual encounter with both of them,. My oldest son stopped things from going too far, regardless of his being intoxicated, and they left the fort, walked over to his buddy's home to stayed there for the remainder of the weekend.

My son never told me about this until 2005. I will elaborate more on this later in my book.

When I finally did get the chance to ask him why he hadn't told me, he said that he was too embarrassed. I had really hoped that I had built a trust solid enough between the two of us that he could tell me ANYTHING, but I had failed to do so and both of my sons had suffered the consequences.

2002

As you all know by now, I am a highly sexual person. Both sexes have been an eye catcher for me but I am also a one-person woman. Sex between Bill and I was okay. We were more into foreplay than the real act itself.

Bill and I decided to go to the "TOY" store and browse around for things that would enhance our love life. I perused through the clothing and the candles thinking this and that would help.

Bill walked over to me and said, "Come here, I want to show you something." I got a little excited and said, "Okay!!" I'm sure I was grinning ear to ear at that time as well.

We came along to the toy aisle. Bill stood me in front of the dildo section. He pointed to a very large dildo.

I said, "I do NOT want that!"
He replied, "It isn't for you. It's for me!"

I just looked at him???!!!

"What?" I said.
He repeated, "It's for me."

My stomach dropped, I wanted to puke all over him!
Damn him!!

I ejected myself from the store and lit a cigarette. I couldn't even think straight!

About 10 minutes go by and Bill walks out with this big bag full of "goodies" and who knew what else at the time and we rode home in silence.

Now, I will tell you this, if you love someone, I guess, you please them in whatever way they feel they need...... so I tried..... until I was so disgusted with this act and the aftermath that I had to call the relationship quits.

I moved out pretty quickly after that...........

2003

After moving out of Bill's home, I put a down payment on a town home in a small complex complete with a pool, clubhouse, and was situated just near the mall and park for my sons. My hard work had paid off and I was a home owner once again! I was elated. The community welcomed us to their best ability. I was the only owner who had children and the noise of my sons at the pool sometimes got on the neighbors' nerves. Everyone living there was settled, older, or retired. We all had eventually learned to co-exist and things were going well.

In 2004, I had also decided that I was done with men and began dating women exclusively. What a roller coaster that was. I did not make good decisions during the four years that I was involved with women and will never return to that world. It was exciting at first. Playing on women's softball teams, partying, the sex was good with basically one of the women that I had dated. I had noticed that I was able to give pleasure but was never able to fully be reciprocated as needed. I wasn't frustrated very often as I am more a giver than a taker. Miss A was a firecracker and very ADHD. She was a Physical Education teacher at a middle school and I was enamored with her energy and vitality. She was also cute as a button and had an infectious smile. She played on a women's football team in Portland. The games were exciting and the after parties even better. The thing that broke us up was that she wanted kids and I was not interested in raising any other kids other than my own.

The following months, I dated a police officer who ran me as hard as her cadets. We went to the gym daily and ran on weekends. I was tired a lot but kept up with her to please her. We also worked out at her home. She was a good person but sexually void and had demons in her own closet. When Tonya was a small girl, she had walked in on her mother proceeding to blow her own head off with a gun. I cannot even imagine what Tonya had gone through but she became a woman who could not connect emotionally with others and I had become a communicator.

I had booked a trip to Vegas to meet my half-sister, and prior to going, Tonya had gone away for a weekend seminar. When she returned, she stated that she had met someone and asked if we could see other people. Now, I do not share, at all. She asked if she could still go to Vegas with me and I replied that she could not. I broke it off with her. I was in the process of buying her truck from her and gave it back, even though she said that I could keep the truck and disregard the remaining payments that I owed her. That was the end of that.

I did not spend the time at home with my boys as I am sure that they needed and I do regret that very much. Juggling work and school made it difficult to keep the reins on my sons.

They had all the free time they wished for and Wayne was losing his way quickly in school and partying all the time. He chose to go live with his best friend's family and I allowed it as he was becoming a bit abusive towards his brother. I paid the family a monthly salary to house Wayne and keep him in school.

I decided to return to college to become a nurse.
I should have waited until after they were grown. A single parent family is hard enough without trying to fit a life of your own in the equation.

2005

Work and school were both going well. I went head strong to obtain my medical degree. I was sent, for my internship, as the first student to be an ER technician prior to graduating at the largest hospital in Clark County, Washington. What an honor! Once graduated with my Associate's Degree, I was offered a paying position at the hospital but was told that I needed to obtain my CNA certification, which I did, and went back to the hospital to gain employment, only to be told that there weren't any open positions at that time. I was floored, discouraged, and needed to regroup. I then went back to school to receive my Bachelor's Degree but had seen that my time away from my kids needed to be more in depth as I had lost them during my hard work to gain better employment, a larger paycheck, and take better care of my sons.

During this time, my friend Mary had announced that she was engaged to a man in the Marines. It was Daniel, the man I had met years before. At this time, I had not known what had transpired between Daniel and Wayne. I knew nothing and was merely happy to have my friend, who was also my classmate, living near my family. They were seeking housing in our area and I had found a rental within walking distance to which they then rented and we hung out all of the time. They had a key to my house and were a tight part of our family unit.

One evening, Daniel had asked to take my boys to a monster truck show. I thought that was a great idea and Mary and I would go have a girls' night out and go dancing.

As the evening ended, Mary had stayed at my home. I thought everyone was asleep in their rooms and that Daniel had dropped my boys off safely at home. The next morning, my oldest came to me and told me that Keith had just walked in, could barely breathe, and had said that Daniel had molested him. I screamed for everyone to call 9-1-1 as I ran to

Keith to collect my son and his information. Keith was in tears and was not making any sense, his words were garbled, and he reeked of alcohol. I then ran out of the house to Daniel's place and told him I had called the cops. "You are going down! How could you do this?!!!" I had screamed at Daniel. He asked if there was something we could work out... *What the hell did that mean?!!* I turned to leave and ran into my oldest, who was holding a baseball bat in hopes, I'm sure, of beating this guy's brains out. I grabbed Wayne and we ran back home.

I gathered Keith into my arms and held him until a copious amount of police showed up to get Keith's statement and to also speak with my oldest. Once the police had taken their statements is when my oldest son told me of the accounts of the evening in the fort with Daniel. He told me he didn't say anything because he was embarrassed and I had then lost it in tears and pain for what my sons had encountered and that I was a failure to my sons, once again.

The police arrested Daniel and he sat in county jail, without bail until he was sentenced to seven years in prison for the crimes he had committed against my family. It took 18 months to convict him and my family and I went through hell while waiting and going to counseling to help my boys get through their trauma. I had also found out that Daniel had molested three other boys in Louisiana after Katrina had hit and while he was stationed there to protect our country. This man did not deserve to breathe but I let the courts handle it and hoped that seeing Daniel put away would help my sons have some closure. Everything my boys had gone through brought all of my demons back into play. My counseling went on for a year, while the boys just refused to speak to their counselors and nothing was accomplished for them. It must be agony for a boy to go through being molested, as, I believe, it is easier for girls and women to discuss abuse than it is for boys and men because of how we are raised.... men to be strong and capable providers and women were to be homemakers and the emotionally stable Mom. I needed to play all roles and did not do well at any of them, I feel.

I immediately got our family into individual counseling. I was dealing with what I was going through and taking time off of work to transport my sons to their continued counseling. I had hoped that this would help them cope as well and begin their healing process.

I asked the District Attorney what had happened to my children and he explained to me that my sons did not want me to know. To this day, I do not know what happened, which gives me the worst thoughts in my head, sends shivers down my spine, and sometimes I can barely breathe while experiencing these emotions.

While deciding what I was going to do next, my youngest son had begun battling school. Keith had been caught with pot on campus and charged with a felony. He was so distraught that I could not even punish him. I knew why he had gotten into drugs— to fade out— and I just tried to support him in any way that I possibly could. He was not expelled as I spoke to his counselor and the principal as to what had happened to my son and that we would work hard to keep him on a tight rein and get him to walk among his class mates with a tassel and gown. Keith did the work, I supervised and we met with his counselor every week. Keith accomplished the tasks set before him and he graduated with his class. My mother was a sweetheart and flew out to watch him walk across the stage. It was a fine moment for us all.

Summer came and went. The boys were partying and I could not keep up. One evening, the boys came home and Keith had explained to me that his brother had consumed a large quantity of mushrooms and was having a "bad trip." Wayne had just laid with his head on my lap and repeated the word "Mom." I called poison control to ask what to do. I was instructed to feed him and put him a warm bath to let him soak and that would help him "come down" from the hallucinogens.

I stayed in the bathroom with him to make sure he didn't drown but he stayed sitting in the tub with his arms around his legs and let the shower cascade over his body until the hot water became cold. He slept for a very long time after that and did not overdose on any drug following that episode.

Now, Wayne and I had a turbulent relationship since his childhood. His father and I had been long over since he was 2½ but he was angry with me for the separation. I was the bad guy and I couldn't explain, until he was older, why this was. When I explained the situation, that his father chose meth instead of his family, he chose not to believe me. He remained angry with me for most of his childhood, teens, and early adulthood.

While in Wayne's teens, he was angry, abusing drugs and could not stand to be around me. Even while living with his friend, which I though was best since their family was intact, he skipped school religiously and ended up getting his GED, which I was proud of. At least he completed that, it was better than nothing. Wayne was extremely smart and I had hoped that college would be in his future. High school bored him as he was way ahead of his other classmates but chose to ditch school instead of going to a school counselor to get into better classes. He was not an athlete as his brother was and just stuck to doing drugs and trying to find his own identity and place in the world.

I didn't blame him. I had done the same when I was a teen. Rebellious, angry, confused, missing having a two-parent family, skipping school because I was too advanced, and getting my state proficiency certification. It was deja vu!

He enjoyed piercings. One day, he came to the house with a safety pin in his cheek. I was floored and told him to remove it. He was not going to pay heed to my rule and we got into it physically. I went to remove the safety pin myself and he pushed me away. Things got pretty heated and he ended up choking me out until I had a seizure. I was in counseling at the time and went to see her to let her know what had happened. She had a police officer come by and he said to go to the ER. I did so and after 3+ hours on a gurney, I was told I simply was experiencing a headache. I was pissed!!

The following year, Wayne and I had once again gotten into an argument, which turned out to be a fight, and he came after me up the staircase, tearing out the banister from the wall, and heading up with his hands in position to choke me. I froze and he just stopped and left the home. I called the cops, showed them the banister, and told them that he had put his hands on me. I lied. I was so angry over tearing up the house and his putting me in fear of my well-being, I just lied. Wayne turned himself in and was sent to juvenile hall. When the center called to tell me to pick him up, I replied, "Keep him another week. I am in fear of my safety and he needs to learn a lesson."

My mother flew up to be a support for him and when she took him to court, instead of my coming to see the judge and explain my side, he just plead guilty to domestic violence and was labeled in the system. I would have perjured myself, giving my side of the story about the previous year and my fear of him, asking for counseling but getting the charge dropped. It was a shame that all that had come down to what it was. He was angry with me for lying but I reminded him of the seizure he had caused me the prior year and that a lesson was needed to be learned. We didn't have any altercations after that.

Wayne did not stay long at the home after that. He moved out when he was 18 and went to live with a woman who was very toxic for him. A 60+ year old woman who had an intense crush on him. She called him by her ex-husband's name, gave him gifts and money, put up with his shit, and even fed him copious amounts of alcohol to try and seduce him. It worked a few times and we all knew it.

While working for this woman, who owned a fast-food restaurant, every employee was a teenager and they were all having sex with one another. I don't know how they all survived that way but they did. This place was a never-ending shit show full of drama and dysfunction and the owner encouraged

130

their behavior and loved the drama as she had no life of her own. Both my boys were employed there and stayed working for her for nearly 7 years.

2008

In February of 2008, I was employed as an office manager at a metal fabrication shop. I was in my third year of nursing school. I became bored of nothing to do after I had done my office duties and went to learn the welding side of the business. Driving a forklift and learning the different machines in the shop was awesome! I learned how to spot weld, use a piranha to cut metal, the wet saw, and I was pretty happy.

In May, while driving the forklift with a huge beam, I was backed into by another forklift driver and the crash broke my lower spine, literally.

It wasn't until November that Worker's Compensation for the state of Washington had allowed my back to be fused and rehabilitation started. I had no college or career to look forward to any longer. My life was shit.

During this time, I had become addicted to my pain medication, Percocet. Addiction takes a toll in many ways and can have serious repercussions. By the end of the year, when this drug no longer worked, my neighbor introduced me to Oxycontin and I was amazed at the euphoric feeling I had. No more pain, only bliss.

Sherry and I were not just neighbors. We were also on our condominium's association as president and treasurer.

My neighbor would crush it up and we would snort it. At first, I couldn't handle the high and would throw up immediately. After a few days, this no longer happened and we began consuming a pill a day and then two at $17 per pill, per person. This was going to break me in many ways down the road as you will soon learn.

In the summer of 2009, I began going to NA meetings to break this addiction and get my life back in order... this would bear fruit in my recovery, but I would have to endure some hardships for my shortcomings as well.

In fall of 2009, my Mom gifted me with a Mother and Daughter vacation to Italy. We spent time in Florence, Venice, and Rome. It was a magical time and my mother and I became closer than ever, sharing this experience and sharing our love for one another. My mother's struggles as a child made it hard for her to be a nurturing mother, but she made up for it in many ways. She had always made every holiday special for us. We took vacations whenever she could afford to. I do have many fond memories of her that I have not written about. These I will keep close to my heart forever. As a single mother, she strove to be the best she could with what she had, regardless of the adversities that she herself had to endure and overcome.

Upon returning home from our trip, I began proceedings on getting my life back in order, making amends for my wrong doings with the condo association's books and repaying the funds that Sherry and I had used up over the past year or so.

I spent 77 days in work release and when I got out, I had no home to live in as I was ousted from my home by the judge.

In September of 2010, after my stay in work release, I was free to resume life, released without probation or any other repercussions except for the fact that I was homeless.

During this time, Daniel was released early from jail because of good behavior. I was planning in my head to hurt Daniel and then hurt myself. I had to get away from Clark County for a while and get my head together.

Since I had no home to go to, regardless of couch surfing, I decided to go to California and remodel my mom's house for the time being, just to clear my head and obtain a new game plan for our lives. We still had the condo and my sons were to make the small house payments while I paid the association dues and all would be well.

My oldest son decided to bail to Colorado with his girlfriend and Keith was left alone at age 19. I asked him to come to California and be with me while I got counseling and worked on my folk's home and he chose to stay at the condo alone and keep working.

In mid-October, Wayne called me in such distress and asked me to go get him from Colorado. I did not have all the funds to do so but met him in Utah and we drove back together. Upon our return, I was able to track down his dad and at least attempt to get him back into his sons' lives, to no avail.

Wayne and I got a wild hair up our asses and decided we were going to drive up to Washington to surprise my youngest. As we arrived, Keith was definitely not happy to see a man that he barely knew walk into his home and try to give him hugs. I don't blame him one bit. I should have called to see if it was okay for this to happen and all that came about was another grievance filed in his mind against me. I thought it would be healing for all three of them but I was wrong.

While their dad was visiting, I had come to the conclusion that my life was over, my boys' dad was there now, and I could go to sleep and not wake up.

I felt it was best for all if I was no longer in the picture. I chose, for the third time, to take my life. My boys' dad was there, the condo was there, everyone would be safe and housed, and I was tired. Too tired to be around, too tired of trying and failing, too tired of being me. Too tired of being a failure as a mother and person.

I swallowed my newly filled 3-month supply of various pills, approximately 180 pills. I took every one of them. I left note after note apologizing, saying it was not my boys' fault and that I was tired. I wrote that I was hoping their dad would pick up the pieces and step up to the plate for once in his life as a father. I felt I was better off dead and then I wouldn't cause anyone else anymore troubles or heart ache.

Wayne was able to break through the motel door and seeing the empty pill bottles, the notes, and my being non-responsive proceeded to shove his fist down my throat to make me vomit. He threw me into the shower to attempt to revive me and somewhere, I am not sure how, he obtained charcoal and shoved that down my throat as well. They drove me to the ER and dropped my failed ass off.

Needless to say, neither of them spoke to me for quite some time after that.

Also, to point out, the boys' dad did not stick around. He ran home to jump back into the meth pipe so as not to have to deal with the caring or comfort of his sons. Piece of SHIT! Yeah, I may have been doing a fucked-up thing by bailing out and attempting to get their dad to step up, but I had tried to do so many times while we were in Washington. I was making really good money (prior to my work injury) and offered to pay their dad's rent, even if he brought his girl up with him, and to support his ass just so he'd have a decent relationship with his sons.

Six days later, I woke from a coma and there was my mother standing by my side as I say loudly, "Mamma!" I had regained consciousness without much brain damage.

My mother told me that all the nurses started crying and were so happy that I had come out of the coma, they even sent me a letter to my mother's home after I had been in recovery for a few weeks back at Mom's place.

I stepped into recovery and counseling for 15 months, three times a week. It did a world of good for me. I was put on an antidepressant and an anti-anxiety pill, which I still take to this day. My counselor pushed me to talk about my entire life, to draw pictures of the nightmare that I had when I was very young, pictures of places where I was harmed, and places that made me happy. She bought me a hand-held voice recorder to clear my head of all the shit that ran around in there, trying to tell me to let go of my past life but also to remind me that maybe I was a three-time loser with suicide attempts, BUT ALSO TO REMIND ME THAT I WAS A SURVIVOR IN EVERY ASPECT OF MY LIFE AND I WOULD PREVAIL.

2011

I continued counseling and obtained a part-time job at a Chiropractic office in January. I was still working on my mom's home at the time, doing the finishing touches, when my neck and arms had become so weak that I couldn't even hold a pencil. In May, I went to see a neurologist, had an MRI, and was told that I needed surgery. The neurologist stated that I had the neck of a 70-year-old woman and a 7-level fusion, C3-T2 was going to be needed.

I have been told since then that only 3 levels should be done at one time, but this doctor felt he could accomplish all of this in one sitting. My operation lasted 10 hours. I did not heal right as the orderlies failed to put my hard collar on to stabilize me when they ambulated me to use the rest room. My neck fell to one side and I heard a crack so loud that my parents heard it from across the room.

My mother went directly to the hospital administrator to chew him out. She wanted to get an attorney and I wish that she would have.

After two weeks, I returned to the Neurologist and he noted that just by touching my back, it looked as though I was an uncovered waterbed, bubbles of fluid were actually seen moving around beneath my skin in my upper back. He sent me straight to the ER and they drained over 730cc's of fluid from my cervical spine. I was then admitted to the hospital again and placed on antibiotics intravenously for two weeks. While in the hospital, the IV in my vein in the crook of my elbow had pulled out some and I rang to tell her.

She dismissed this and said that it was fine. The antibiotics were draining onto my arm and I ended up getting phlebitis, which caused my arm to swell up and feel as if it would explode. They released me like that and said to put hot compresses on it. I returned to the ER two days later because I had only gotten worse. I was then admitted again and went back into the operating room. They opened me back up again and cut more of my tissue out that they considered compromised from the excess fluid that had accumulated in my back and placed a wound vac, a vacuum, onto my back to suck any more excess fluid out and to close my wound as they did not place any more stitches in my back.

I had a home health nurse come to my mother's home every other day to clean the wound with large Q-tips, debride the tissue to bring the healthy tissue back up to the surface, and replace the vacuum onto my 5-inch gaping wound. My mother was so into blood and guts, as was I, that she took photos to show me. It was a trip! When my nurse returned to clean my wound, I asked if I could touch my wound, as my spine and spinal cord were completely uncovered except for the sheath that covered it for protection.

He said that I could do so, and I reached back and touched it, felt the length of cord that was exposed and how far up into my skull my wound opened up to. I literally went into my lower cranium and instead of being grossed out I was utterly fascinated! My mother took pictures during my healing process and I posted them to my Facebook page.

The vacuum was left on me for four months. I then had to have a pic line, which is a line that went from an artery in my arm straight to my heart, and I was to inject six types of antibiotics into this pic line twice a day. The lines hung from my right arm and we kept them wrapped up in gauze as I moved around the house.

When I felt well enough to go out of the house, I went to see one of my favorite musicians, Paul Rodgers, in concert. As I sat in the back area during the concert, I uncovered my lines and proceeded to inject my antibiotics towards my heart, re-wrapped my arm, and continued to enjoy the concert. I had met a guy there who was fascinated by what I was doing, came to sit with me, and listened to my story.

Come to find out this guy knew the drummer of the band and got me back stage to meet Paul and his band mates! I had pictures taken and put them up on Facebook beaming with pleasure over this gift I had been given, which somehow made being sick worth it. A memory I will cherish forever!

The wound vac had done all it could by late November 2011 and my upper back had closed around my 6th vertebrae. The bone was completely exposed. My nurse made silly fun of me and said my neck looked liked a vagina! I laughed yet was mortified at the same time as I reached around and literally felt what he described to me and then asked to have a photo shown to me to view the anomaly. My mom took the photos and I couldn't believe what that vac had done and knew that another operation was needed. My neurologist said there wasn't much he could do and deemed me permanently disabled. He recommended a Plastic Surgeon to help me and after several visits, the Plastic Surgeon came together with my Neurologist and back into the operating room I went.

November 11th, 2011, the Plastic Surgeon and my Neurologist opened my upper back once again, took my two trapezoid muscles, which is what we all have in our backs, just two muscles, filleted them into six pieces and laid them in a way to cover up my c-spine and closed me back up. Another pic line was introduced to my artery and heart for two weeks and I was done with all surgeries, or so I had hoped.

Michele Desmond

I healed pretty well and now have a huge, ugly divot in my neck that "wows" all who view it. I am debating getting a Mandela tattoo to cover up the scar but have been told that it is sexy and shows the strength I have by enduring such a traumatic year. I've been called a trooper, a "Mutant," a freak of nature, and a phenomenal survivor from all I have endured in life and they are glad that I am writing about all of this. At this moment in time, I am glad I am doing so as well.

By mid-2012, I was ready to move on as my step dad had displayed days of abuse towards my mother and I couldn't contain myself any longer. I got in his face and when he then threatened to hurt me, I shoved him thinking of the time that my mother had come to live with me in Washington after being beaten by his own hands.

My mother endured over 20 years of abuse at the hands of this man and I came to the conclusion that I would end up killing this man if I ever saw him put his hands on her. One evening, he was in her face and I got between them and literally told him that if he ever touched my mother in anyway besides out of love, I would kill him. He then kicked me out of the house. I begged my mother to leave with me, explaining to her that I would never return under any circumstance.... She stayed.

It was then that I knew I had to leave soon or I would hurt him.

In August of 2012, I took a train to surprise my sons and stayed two weeks. I felt like I was more of an inconvenience than anything else. My youngest was working and my eldest was getting loaded all the time. I felt more lonely being there than if I had stayed back at my mom's place. At least I had my dog with me to keep me company.

Our town home had defaulted in 2011 and it was lost to a short sale so my sons were living in an apartment located across town.

During my visit with my boys, my half-sister, Charlene, who lived in Arkansas, called me to say that her best friend and ex-girlfriend had been shot to death. She asked me to come out and stay with her in Arkansas. I agreed to do so as it was time to leave the abuse in California.

When I arrived back at my mother's place, I loaded up my car with whatever would fit, spent the last few days with my sweet mother and drove away to Arkansas to fix yet another person instead of going back to Washington, which is what I should have done. I still had the urge to hurt the man who molested my sons. I wasn't ready to be near that area yet.

I arrived at my sister's home in 28 hours to love and support her. I was still working with my attorney to get put on disability while doing what I could so I didn't feel like a mooch at Charlene's place. I cooked, cleaned, did her laundry, ironed, and walked A LOT.

My sister was into a religion that I did not believe in. She was/is a Jehovah's Witness and she shoved books in my face to attempt to convert me, even though she was ousted from her own church because she was a lesbian.

When we would attempt to go out and play pool or to karaoke, people would think we were a couple and I soon became very tired of trying to explain that we were sisters, so we stopped going out. One evening while we were drinking at home and listening to music, my sister grabbed me to dance with her which I thought nothing of, and in a moment that I wish had never happened, she made an attempt to kiss me while proceeding to say that this was a relationship that could work out because we were only half-sisters. I pulled away and said if she ever did that again, I would leave and she would never see me. She blamed it on the alcohol and said it would never happen again.

Soon after that, I hopped onto an online dating site, I believe to get the hell out of that living situation, as things had become very strained between the two of us, and met a man who I spoke with online for over months.

In January of 2013, I decided it was a good time to meet this man in person, I did not know what he looked like as aesthetics were a trait I took into consideration first, as well as sex, so I felt I was doing the right thing. After over three months of chatting online and then speaking on the phone, I drove 80 miles to meet him in Joplin, Missouri at a Denny's restaurant. Upon arriving, I discovered this man weighed nearly 400 lbs. and it freaked me the hell out but I kept telling myself this was my best friend and I needed to change my ways and believe I was being healthy with this decision of getting together with a different type of person.

This man, who lived with his 12-year-old son in Baxter Springs, Kansas, became my husband 10 months later. I did this for him. I did not want to get married but he truly was my best friend and it was a beautiful ceremony. I felt like a princess for a day. My mother became ordained and I was proud to have her marry us. She gave us a Native American blessing, as my heritage includes QUAPAW (Ogawa) Sioux. I still have the gown that she wore when she attended the wedding. I hope I made her proud that day. She liked who I was with even though I was so far away and in Tornado Alley.

She came to visit and we went on a road trip to see her ancestors burial grounds, her cousins, and visit every area that she knew her full blooded grandmother had lived and been to. I loved spending that time with her and it reminded me of the closeness we once felt when I lived with her back in 2010-2012.

After I was married, I went to visit my half-sister for a day while my husband was away at a conference. Speaking with my half-sister while visiting with her one weekend, she told me of how she had oral sex with my father, who I will call my sperm donor, because he does not deserve to be called my father from him molesting me at the age of two. My sister had told me that this sexual contact had been when she was 16 and that he had been molesting her most of her life. I was floored and after returning home, I wrote and told her that I never wanted to see her ever again. I am ashamed and appalled that I belong to such a disgusting family on my sperm donor's side.

What did I have in common with my family except to be related to a pedophile who molested all of his girls except my youngest sister who was only 5 months old when my mother took off with us in the middle of the night while my sperm donor was out gallivanting around.

2013-2015

Married life was boring with added drama that I did not want or need. We lived as boring married people did. My husband lost 112 pounds the first year we were together and then decided he wanted to be morbidly obese again, as the rest of his family was.

It was strange how, during late fall until early summer came, this man just wanted to work, come home, and eat. During the summer and into fall, we would camp in our motor home and take road trips. Other than that, there was absolutely nothing going on in our world.

I had fallen into HIS lifestyle and was losing myself again. I had gained a good 40 pounds. I was not happy. I did not want to live this way and the marriage began to slowly ebb into nothingness.

2016 -2018

2016 was a difficult year.

The year started out quite complacent. My marriage was winding down and we barely spoke.

My step son had a game room, which was separated from the house and attached to the garage. I knocked on the door and when he opened it, I discovered two girls and another guy friend of his barely waking up. There were empty booze bottles all over the place and I was livid. My step son was 15 by then and I wasn't about to play that shit all over again. I told my husband, Jim, what had gone down and my step son denied the entire scene, calling me a liar! *Oh, hell no!* Jim actually took the side of my step son and I was done trying to live a life that I was unhappy in.

In March, I had found out that my husband was having an affair and decided to file for divorce.

During that time, I was awaiting surgery for my lower spine. A fusion was to be done from L2 to S1... a revision from my 2008 surgery.

This was to ensue on July 5th.

My husband was trying to evict me from our home two weeks prior to that so that I would have nowhere to go! My lawyer had the judge give me a 30 day stay in the home and I was to vacate by the end of July. I had to have surgery and then worry about moving out. So while awaiting my surgery, I had to move my belongings into a storage unit all by myself.

What I had left in the home were boxes of important things that I hadn't put into storage yet and when I returned to the house, my husband was sitting on the porch with his whole family and his ex-wife who he had been having an affair with for the last 10 months! What a class act that was!

I had an order to have him leave and retain the home in my name for the next 30 days…. I went to the cops to have this paperwork served and they were lackadaisical about it as lazy cops can be in a Podunk town... So I told the cops I was going to serve it myself. Then they got off their asses and served him themselves. It takes a bitch to make things happen sometimes. And I was tired of taking crap from men who thought they could control my life, damn it!

So, the surgery happened, I was in the hospital for three days and then I was told no lifting more than five pounds…. Here's the kicker... the only friends I had were made through my husband so I was left with no one….

I had to do this by myself. So I took a week to recover and strapped on a huge, torso sized, back brace and began to once again move my shit into storage.

During this time, I searched for roommates that I could afford to move in with. The first one was an old pervert who wanted to rub my feet while interviewing me. Scratch that!

The next guy had a huge home in a country setting with horses and a serene environment... I moved in after giving rent and deposits and two days later I was told that if I slept with him, he would reduce my rent to nothing.

So, the next day, I rent a U-Haul and ask my son to help me move the hell out of there. The dude tried to keep my large flat screen tv as well as my rent. I left with the television and told him to keep the money. Pick my battles, right?

I then look on a well-known site, Craigslist, to look for someone needing a roommate. I go to a shitty part of town to look at a room that was of good size but lacked a door.... the entrance to the room was a heavy blanket to which he said he would have a door framed in... which he never did. I was at my last straw, strapped for cash because most of my money was tied up in a piece of shit attorney for my divorce.

So I rented the room. The old dude wanted $450 a month.... with no bedroom door, a bathroom I have to share with this guy, and to add to the bullshit, he has a friend come over during our interview and pulls out a bag of weed from his freezer and handed it to this visitor.

So, in essence, I am moving in with a drug dealer, who later shows himself to be a pervert as well. Could there possibly be anything that CANNOT go wrong with this year? While at this dude's house, I can actually hear him breathing from the other side of the tapestry. Drug traffic came and went at all hours of the day and night and this guy was a deaf gamer so he wore a head set and yelled obscenities nonstop! I felt as though I was losing my mind!

I then decided to take on dog sitting for a friend who lived four hours away from the dude's house and I happily went. I took all that was important to me: my family's jewelry, what little clothes I had, and my dog.

Now I need to tell you that my dog was not just a pet, she was my service dog. Caine was her name. Caine was a great dog, in great health on the west coast. Moving to the mid-west, there are different climates, different grasses, and allergies. Caine became very sick. She lost her hair and became full of edema. I had to take her to the vet every month for an allergy shot. Upon taking this dog sitting position for a month, I had been given two doses of her shots to administer accordingly.

This place that my friends had was on a 5-acre farm. Caine was not only allergic to chicken and grains, she was allergic to GRASS... all types of grass that the Midwest provided her... she continued to get worse, regardless of the medication I was giving to her. She lost the rest of her hair and developed tumors on her spine.

The day before it was time to go home, I went to the airport to pick up my friends and when we returned, the entire house was engulfed in flames.....*What the hell had I done to make this happen?* I felt cursed! It turned out, finding later, that my friends and their neighbor were having a serious war over the land lot lines and a shadow of a person was seen on the back deck where the fire had started, according to the fire department.

While the fire is ensuing, we are running around looking for our dogs among the fire and smoke... a neighbor down the road was there and told us that he had heard Caine barking and busted out the front window to save the animals.

So now, not only has my girl got tumors, no hair, allergies that are killing her, but now she is burned badly and has smoke inhalation.....

Not only had I lost EVERYTHING that meant anything to me, but my dog was going to leave me as well. I knew it in my heart....

I drove home the next day and spent the evening cuddling my dog and took her to the vet the next day to see if there was something we could do to help her... He said the tumors were extensive and wasn't sure he could fix what ailed her. I said that I was so tired of seeing her in pain and agony that I wanted to let her go to heaven. We all prayed with her then he let me hold her as he put her to sleep.... Afterwards, I just drove for hours through Kansas. I couldn't even think straight. I just wanted to die.

So divorce, dysfunctional roommates, drug dealing perverts, a house fire to which I lose everything, my dog passes, and I'm going to be homeless when I get back to Joplin all because I gave my notice that I was leaving the environment he was putting me in.

Arriving back to the dude's house, I had seen that all my things that I had stored under the outside enclosed carport had been crammed in to my room and there was another guy sleeping on the couch that was in between my room, the dude's room, and to get to the bathroom.

It turned out that this guy was the dude's nephew that had recently been kicked out of his own home for cheating on his wife of 16 years with the 19-year-old nanny.

I still had to move out. The dude gave me a month without any rent added to my bill because of Caine's passing to give me time to relocate. In the meantime, I dove head first into a relationship with the dude's nephew. Not a good decision!

I decided to try a female to live with his time. I went to her house for a one-on-one interview. We seemed to jive pretty well, then her boyfriend walks out of the bedroom, to which I had no idea he was there, and then she proceeds to tell me that he stays there most of the time.

Her boyfriend's energy freaked me the hell out! Yet, I had nowhere else to turn so I took the room and started moving in the next day. Having my car loaded up with a lot of my shit, I meet a utility guy getting ready to turn the electric off! I paid the $80 bill just to keep the lights on…. and this is after I had given Tina $600 just for moving in!

So, Tina reimbursed me a few days later... I learned within days that Tina's boyfriend is a heavy drinker and an abuser. This I would have to deal with for the time being and hope things would mellow out. Tina and I seemed to work well together and I was pretty content when her boyfriend was not there. Turns out, he was there more often than not. So, I just invited my own train wreck over as often as possible myself. At least he kept the peace.

Three weeks later, I moved out because Tina's boyfriend is a woman batterer. I saw it with my own eyes. He had even gotten in my face threatening to beat my ass! I got a police report for that evening and obtained a restraining order on him the next day. A week goes by and a sheriff came to the door and actually served me with a restraining order by Tina because she attested that I brandished gun in her boyfriend's face! I've never even owned a gun! When I go to fight this restraining order, Tina and her boyfriend never even showed up!

So I ended up paying nearly $800 bucks to stay at a place for just about 3 weeks……

I found an extremely small apartment down the street from the dealer's home.

My relationship with his nephew, Will, continued and I, at the very least, had something to take my mind off of all the crap I had endured the past few years by having someone fun but totally dysfunctional.

I still didn't know if I was coming or going. I was nearing 50, lost, and I truly missed my family. I didn't feel at home anywhere but I did know where my heart belonged.. with my sons. Yet, I still felt very out of place whenever I visited Washington because of the travesty that occurred to my kids and the man who committed these acts that resides less than 40 minutes away from them.

During that year, I decided that my sexual life was one of complacency. I entered into the world of BDSM through a website and was contacted by a Master to see if I could learn to be a submissive or a slave.

The acts were quite therapeutic, as crazy as that sounds. I learned what "sub space" was about and found that I could "zone out" the pain and feel the feelings of where my actual emotional pain was coming from. I cried my eyes out after the sessions and worked through a lot of the anger and hatred I had for my past marriage and the people that had hurt me and my boys. It sounds intense, and believe me when I say it is, but I prevailed and after six months, determined that this life was not my cup of tea but that I had actually survived another crucial part of my journey and returned back to my place of dwelling to recover and get on with my life.

I will leave that part of my journey and my three years with Will to my next book… There is a lot that needs to be said there and this is not the novel to write about it in.

The one thing that I absolutely can tell you is that my relationship with Will drained me of all that I had left in my being to withstand abuse, lies, and neglect. I gave everything I had to this man and it was all for naught. I loved the idea of loving him and of his NEEDING me, but I was not who he wanted. He proved that time and time again. So when that bubble burst, so did I.

This caused me to make a stand for MYSELF and end the dysfunction. I had decided I no longer wished to ever enter into another relationship. I was resolved to living alone for the rest of my life because it was safe. I had finally became MY OWN true friend and found a peace within that I had been missing for so long. I welcomed the serenity of my own time and found ME.

2017

My mother is dying.... In January, she was diagnosed with an idiopathic pulmonary disease. They took a biopsy and sent it off to the CDC and the UK to have it tested so that maybe they can help others in the future if a cure is found. The CDC came and even quarantined her when she was in the hospital. She stayed in the hospital from December to the end of January. The specialists asked her if she was raised on chicken farm... she was not. They called it "Popcorn Lung" but they couldn't even pin point what the hell it was that she had.

Mom was given 3-6 months to live. I was going to lose my best friend.

In March, she asked me to come and spend time with her, which of course I did. I wish I would have stayed longer. It was unfortunate because I was so tired from being strapped of emotional stability for her and myself. We played Scrabble, as we always did since I was 12 years old. I even have that original board game that she taught me on....

My Mom was on steroids to keep her breathing stable so she was a tad aggressive, as steroids can do that to our entire family. She had a mouth on her like a sailor at moments and she and my step dad got into an argument. I'm sitting at the dining room table while they are commencing to exchange words and my step dad, Mike, walks out of the den and pulls my mother's air hose from her breathing machine so my mom couldn't get her oxygen. This is the type of thing that Michael liked to do, a sense of controlling behavior that had always been in their marriage for 27 years. What a disgusting human being! I ran up to the machine and put the air hose back in place and restarted the machine. I should have called the cops! Someone should have pulled HIS air tube out of his fucking lungs! I'll never forget about that nor will I ever forgive him for that last play of abuse that I saw him act out.

Mom made preparations for her passing.. She signed DNR (Do Not Resuscitate) paperwork, obtained a DNR bracelet, and began dividing things up for my sister and I to keep or distribute to her grandchildren. She also chartered a yacht with the Neptune Society.

Mom explained that her passing was to be celebrated, that she would still be all around us and we were to play Bob Marley and drink mimosas while they spread her ashes out to sea in Newport Harbor in California.

I slept a lot in a bed right next to her recliner, which she remained in for most of the rest of her days. I fed her, bathed her, and we played Scrabble together. She was so embarrassed during bathing and bathroom moments. I'm not sure if it was because of her being in her birthday suit or that she was so weak and couldn't do those things for herself, as she was an amazingly independent woman who I admired so greatly. When it was time for me to leave, I didn't want to go…... I cried all the way to the airport and all the way home on the plane. I don't even remember driving home from Tulsa airport, which was nearly two hours away..

Two days after arriving back in Missouri, my mother texted me and asked if I would come back and take care of her. I told her that I would. When I called and asked to be placed on speaker phone with Michael, myself, and my mother, I stated that I would be coming out for my mother. I had then stated specifically to Michael that I did not want to ever see him pull Mom's air hose out again nor did I want to see any abuse from him towards her. He automatically flew off the handle and Mom had to hang up. She sent me an email the next day saying that maybe it wasn't a good idea that I come out after all. I wish I had driven out and done as she asked, regardless of the abuse I knew was to come because I had stood my ground... but I did it over the phone. I should've waited until I was already there beside my mother, but I probably would've gotten kicked out of the home. Who knows? All I do know is that I will never forgive myself for not taking care of her until her final breath.

Michele Desmond

My sons went to visit her for a week and she went downhill fast about two days before they left. The following day after they went home, my mother passed away. She held on like the fighter that she was and made it clear that she was in control of how long she would hang on and she succeeded. I love you Mom.

We carried out her wishes...We spoke dearly of her and what an incredible human being she was, giving herself to all of us, and not really ever asking anything in return. I still feel her at times and my sister says she dreams of her often. I love you Mom. I'm sorry I wasn't there at the end like you had wished for and I hope Michael's karma hits him fast and hard someday.

So, as I write this, I am feeling a pain greater than I have ever known. I don't want to leave my apartment. I am huddled in a fetal position most of the time with aches and pains of life and death and hurt and betrayal that I just can't see myself going around anyone or ever being in a relationship ever again.

I don't want to grow old alone but I have a sense that I will, and that is somewhat okay with me. I won't have to take care of anyone and I can rest and write. I do not trust or like people, truth be told.. I believe most people have forgotten the definition and carrying out of "Common Sense" and "Compassion."

I, at times, feel like I have rejoined the forces of the dysfunctional world without a way out that I can see. I am hoping that my life will not return to the emotional instability that manages to overtake my senses, but I promised my mother that I would never hurt myself again and hold on to my reasons to live: my sons, and now, my grandchildren.

I do not feel suicidal. However, I could very easily wish at times that I would go to sleep only to never wake up again... It was just a passing thought from time to time, as I had promised my mother that I would be all right because of HER...

Near the closing of the year 2017, I had decided that relationships were no longer going to be a part of my life and I settled in to the fact that I might just as well grow old alone. I was safer that way. I found I was seeking love in all the wrong places and getting to the point where I loved MYSELF was most important. Loving myself would put all of the pieces together. I wish I had this epiphany decades ago and saved my family and myself from a lot of bullshit.

It was then that I started spending much time alone. Writing, walking, and a little kayaking when my body would allow. Spending time in the forest and on the river gave me a new perspective. Spending time alone was hard at first but then became a necessity.

Doing things alone had no meaning, until one day I realized that I did not have to worry about anyone but myself. I did not have to answer to anyone but myself. I found a new freedom to which I was master of my own life.

I then began to relish in the peace, MY PEACE, that came quickly after that. I absolutely adored being alone! I spent the next year coming in to the new ME. I liked who I was! I was worthy, responsible, and important. I felt more empowered to reflect and write.

Now, with that being said, I did miss having a canine companion for over a year and a half. Losing my girl, Caine, was devastating and I swore I would never have another dog because she was the perfect companion and NO ONE or nothing would compare to her.

In early 2018, I began perusing through the website of the nearest Humane Society to get a look at possible candidates.

As I scrolled through all of those sweet faces of potential family members, blessings from the universe to give hope and love to whomever adopted them, I saw THE FACE! This pup looked just like my girl Caine and I was entranced with this little guy!

He was five months old and his name at the shelter was Pretzels, a fawn and blue pit mix with adorable, loving eyes and a heart of gold. I checked in on the shelter's website for a week to see if he was still available and then made my move.

Upon entering the shelter, I asked to meet with Pretzels and the attendant drew a HUGE smile on his face! He walked me back to the kennels that held the adoptees and proceeded to tell me how Pretzels was the shelter's favorite dog. The attendant was glowing as he told me of Pretzel's kind demeanor, sensitive style and grace, and that he was timid yet loved being touched. He explained that Pretzels was found at the high school area and had abrasions and marks on his body that resembled having been in fights, or that he could have been a "bait dog" for dog fighting purposes.

We stopped in front of the kennel that held Pretzels and here was this sweet boy, fawn and downy white, with thickened eye liner around his eyes to captivate his audience when he looked at them. His eyes were deep as an old soul, brown like root beer, and with such a sense of longing to be someone's favorite companion. I fell in love instantly!

The attendant took me to a meeting room where he then introduced me personally to Pretzels. This little guy was indeed timid but the moment he walked up to me, I cupped his face in my hands, looked deeply into his gorgeous eyes and we were an item.

He basically melted into me and my tears began to flow. I knew in my heart that this little guy was a gift both from my mother and Caine to add to my peace and joy in my life and to let me know that they are still with me but more tangible than just in spirit. I was blessed!

The adoption went through smoothly and two days later, Pretzels, who I renamed Kane, became my co-pilot and peacekeeper.

Settling in with my new companion, the year went by quickly and I had a new lease on life. I felt complete within my own being and Kane was the icing on top.

In the following years, things began to progress in both fruitful and debilitating ways ….

In summer of 2019, I went on a float trip with friends and was involved in a kayak pile up on the Buffalo river. I ingested far too much water and contracted Klebsiella Pneumonia, pneumonia of the intestines. I was horrible ill for nearly seven months and along with the intestinal pneumonia came a hoard of other problems which took a toll on my health and kept me pretty much bedridden for the rest of the year.

2020-Current

Covid hit and all hell broke loose. I am not one to get into politics or health debates. I am just here to take care of ME. My spirituality has grown immensely. I feel like I have learned many lessons, some I am still walking through, while others are now put away, compartmentalized, and the chapters have nearly closed.

I did receive a long apology from my first husband, Mark, who stated that HE was the problem and felt bad that he couldn't get his shit together while we were together. I accepted his apology and let it go, feeling validated that I had NOT been the crazy one in the relationship.

I had a dream about my father dying and located his number through google to call and check on him. He answered and we spoke about his health. He did tell me that he was indeed dying. I told him that I forgave him for everything and that "we are good." I needed to do that for the both of us so that he could rest in peace and it also helped me to release those years I carried of pain and anger towards him. I knew I was growing up.

Michele Desmond

I have been in a secure relationship for the past 3 years.

I am valuable as a woman, a mother, grandmother and as an individual.
I am RESPECTED.

LOVE IS LOVE

My man is good, kind and generous. When he drinks, my triggers of abuse come up, which I work through. I am not sure where this will lead or if I will stay in this relationship. Only the universe knows. I have become, not religious, but quite SPIRITUAL.

I live alone for the most part while my man is out on the road as an owner/operator of his own trucking company. I rarely go out, except to see my grandchildren as I am back living in Washington state where my family resides. It amazes me of the changes Covid has made, on this state in particular. The homeless population is astounding. There are tents set up along the sidewalks just out front of businesses.

It's unnerving as to the amount of criminal activity that has risen since the pandemic.

In walking my grandkids to our local park, I caught a glimpse of a syringe lying in someone's yard and tears welled up from the sight of this city's demise.

My peace remains intact, for the most part, and I am happy being around my family.

I have been through four surgeries since 2019. My right hip was replaced because the bone became necrotic; it just died on me. I had my right shoulder repaired AGAIN and it has ripped itself apart once again but I will not be having another surgery on it. Twice is enough. My bladder grew a tumor and I had to have it removed along with a hysterectomy and therapy for that.

My last surgery was a titanium fusion from T-8 all the way down to S1. I have barely any range of motion and hurt on a daily basis and my hip is more painful than before it was replaced.

So I am mostly titanium throughout my entire spine. I wish bionic powers came along with the fusion!

Summer will be here soon and I long for the warm days where I can try, if my body will allow it, to get out into my kayak or take a stroll through the woods. The water and forest are my church...

My story is not over....

What the future holds for me is unpredictable. I try not to future trip and attempt to stay in the moment on a daily basis.

I am still learning and still struggling to love.

I do see my sons struggling in their lives due to the problems I had as a child and growing up broken as a parent, a single mother most of the time, and a person learning who I was, then and now. I pray for their struggles to be lighter than my own. I hope for their outcomes to be better and happier in finding themselves in this crazy world we are now enduring.

My oldest son is struggling the most. I am guiding him the best that I can, bringing to the table more insight as a survivor from abuse and addiction, in hopes that this will help him grow.

It is such a struggle for me to see my son caught up in an abusive relationship of his own. He deserves so much better. However, I can relate to how he believes that he doesn't. My best friend, Kelly, says to let go and let God....

He is not walking through this alone as I did. I will not allow that. I do allow him to make the decisions that he does and then we sit and chat, when he reaches out, to work on the next chapter in his life.

It is tragic the way his life is currently, but I am not responsible for his decisions as he is nearly 32 years old now. I can only guide and support as allowed and needed. He is waist deep in dysfunction right now. I will continue to journal about this and hopefully a better outcome will be reached at an earlier age than when my own epiphany came at 50.

I fear for my grandchildren and what their future holds with the potential of World War 3 being a possibility in the years to come and my only wish is that they stay safe, healthy, and happy. I will strive to keep them secure in any way I can.

I am a better grandmother than I was a mother, which is how it came to be with my own mother as she learned from her own struggles and mistakes to be a better caretaker and loving parent/grandparent as she progressed in her own *growing up broken*.

To be continued……..

Knowing then what I know now….

I wonder if I would recognize the difference in my child/grandchild's behavior after they were traumatized? I try to stay alert and open minded about these things now. I try to stay in the present day and acknowledge the energies that surround me.

From experiencing physical and emotional abuse at the hands of people that I was taught to trust, I have come to understand that there are many different ways to talk to and observe our children.

I had no time or functional ability to process the choices I made. Did I know any better? Absolutely not... Crazy was all I knew and had grown up with. Family, teachers, day cares, neighbors.... they all molded me into what I had become from the age of two.

Guilt and regret still haunt me from time to time.

I hope and pray you never have to endure pain like this.

I feel that my mother dealt with my behaviors as a young girl in a way that was disregarded. She wasn't blind but she had blinders on. What parent can fathom that their child has been molested and can see the signs if it hasn't happened to them or they trust everyone around them?

Question everything to a degree!

Back in the 70s, that's probably what went down for most people. Silence was golden, keep "hush-hush" and it will all go away. Child molestation and domestic violence was kept within the household, not spoken about, and swept under the rug.

I missed having PRESENT parents. I needed to be protected. I do not blame my mother for what happened, it was out of her control. She did the best she could with what little she knew in her own upbringing and I thank her for the wonderful times we had. I was lucky to have her, having gone through her own traumas as well and being the strong, capable woman she was, doing the best she could in raising a broken child. She did save me from so many other mistakes I made. She took me in when I was falling and failing. She cared for me when I was bedridden as an adult. She rescued me from myself and took care of me when I felt "done."

I love you Mom!

Many of you will identify with these things that I have written about. Many of us wish we had childhoods we could change.

The people that hurt me, the trauma that I endured and survived, and the distance I felt from myself, I wish I could have changed all of that.

There are some things that I would like to say regarding growing up broken and being a survivor…

A bit of advice I hope you all take into consideration….

Michele Desmond

FAMILIES

Put down your cell phones and tablets! Take time to pay attention to your family and HEAR what they are saying to you. It is a simple step to a rewarding experience if you commit to your family for at least a meal once a day. Technology will always be there but your family will not.

PARENTS

Always be cautious.
Read books on signs of abuse.
Watch for children acting out sexually or being too doting on you as a parent with hugs, cuddles, and kisses.
Observe their behavior for signs of thumb sucking, wetting the bed, acting out on occasions that they normally wouldn't have. The signs will be there, but YOU HAVE TO PAY ATTENTION!
Look for a child who withdraws unexpectedly.
Watch your children's behaviors at family functions.. ANYONE can hurt your children, even those closest to you.
Meet all of your child's friends and their parents as well.
Ask questions – do not make it an inquisition.
Be protective – be overly protective, you can never be too safe.
Teach/help your children to love themselves.

Therapy is ALWAYS helpful, even if it's to have a sounding board.

I know the word "therapy" is not something everyone finds appealing but it can truly help.. IF you are willing to put forth the effort and look at yourself, not just focus on others.

BE AN EXAMPLE

YOUNG ADULTS

When someone offers you alcohol or drugs, remember to say "No thank you" and leave the area. Listen to you "inner self". Trust your gut feelings!
If it doesn't FEEL right to you in your heart and soul, give an excuse to leave, walk away, call your parent(s), go to a friend's home.
Use your cell phone to call for help.
Talk to someone who you trust in every way.
Females can hurt people too, this is not just about a male abuser.
Statically speaking, the closest people to us are the ones who can hurt us the most.
Cry loudly, plead with your abuser, and keep eye contact with them. Call them by their name if you know it.
Fight back!
Do NOT be afraid to be judged when you tell someone.

Your parents are and can be your hero one day if not for all of your life.
Do whatever it takes to keep yourself safe.
Take care of YOU because you are all you have until you reach safety.
We need to cherish and respect OURSELVES first then all else will fall into place.
Remember...one bad decision can wreck your life for years to come.

You will prevail.
You will survive!

I HOPE AND PRAY that you will never have to struggle to love.

Peace and love to all of you!

My next book, ***ON THE MEND*** will be coming someday soon.

Thank you for walking with me through my journey.

www.ingramcontent.com/pod-product-compliance
Lightning Source LLC
Chambersburg PA
CBHW052003090426
42741CB00008B/1533